PRICE A'

EXCLUSIVE PRICE ACTION TRADING APPROACH TO FINANCIAL MARKETS

By LAURENTIU DAMIR

Copyright © 2016 Laurentiu Damir
All rights reserved.

This book is copyright protected. No part of this book may be reproduced, distributed, sold or transmitted in any form or by any means, electronic or mechanical, including photocopying, recording, or any information storage and retrieval system, without prior written permission of the author. Legal action will be pursued if this is breached.

Disclaimer

Please note that the information contained within this document is for educational purposes only. Every attempt has been made to provide accurate, up to date and reliable complete information. No warranties of any kind are expressed or implied. By reading this document, the reader agrees that under no circumstances is the author responsible for any losses, direct or indirect, which are incurred as a result of the use of information contained within this document, including, but not limited to, -errors, omissions or inaccuracies

ISBN-10: 1530176743
ISBN-13: 978-1530176748

TABLE OF CONTENTS

5	CHAPTER ONE – INTRODUCTION
5	WHY HAVE I WRITTEN THIS BOOK ?
6	WHO IS THIS BOOK FOR ?
8	WHY SHOULD YOU READ IT ?
12	HOW WILL THIS IMPROVE YOUR TRADING ?
14	CHAPTER TWO – FAIR VALUE OF PRICE
21	WHAT IS THE FAIR VALUE AREA ?
33	TRADING VOLUME
35	EXCESS PRICE
42	CONTROL PRICE
47	INITIATIVE AND RESPONSIVE TRADING
53	CHAPTER THREE – VALUE SHIFTING
53	MOVING VALUE
58	CONSTRUCTING THE BIG PICTURE
63	VALUE HIGH, LOW AND EXCESS
70	CHAPTER FOUR – USE IN TRADING
70	REJECTION
77	FRAMEWORK
83	TREND IDENTIFICATION AND CHANGE
97	SUPPORT, RESISTANCE, REJECTION
107	CHAPTER FIVE – PUTTING IT TOGETHER
107	TIMEFRAMES
119	SUPPLY AND DEMAND KEY LEVELS

CHAPTER ONE - INTRODUCTION

WHY HAVE I WRITTEN THIS BOOK?

If you are reading this, there is a good possibility that you have read material from me in the past. I wrote a number of short books some years ago explaining my trading ideas and methods.

Those short eBooks had quite a bit of success as it turned out. One of them was actually bestseller in its category for more than 6 months with the others following closely.

I, of course, left my email address for readers to contact me. And that they did. It has been almost four years without writing anything but the emails keep coming every day.

The most popular request I get is to write more about price action, to publish a material where to explain comprehensively the price action techniques I use to trade the markets with. It has taken me quite some time as you see, to follow up on this request.

WHO IS THIS BOOK FOR?

This material assumes the reader has knowledge of basic functionalities of the market or markets he wants to trade.

Things like "how to open up a trade", "how to switch between timeframes" on your trading platform, "how trading with leverage works", "what is a futures contract", "what stocks are best to trade and why" or "what is a forex pair and which are best to trade" will not be covered in this material.

With minimal effort, you can find all this basic information freely on the internet and, to be honest, it will probably be better organized and explained than my version of the same.

I will be focusing solely on technical analysis with price action alone. If you have read one of my books before you are aware of the fact that I do not like to write just for the sake of writing.

My writing style has always been to the point, without any trading stories or redundant information. This might have something to do with the fact that English is not my native language, but the feedback I get is that this concise way of writing is a plus.

Also, I don't like telling stories and speaking off topic in my native language either.

All of this said, if you are at the very beginning with respect to trading, I suggest you do some online searching and acquire basic knowledge of the market or markets you want to start trading.

Familiarize yourself with your trading platform and then come back to reading this book. As well, this material is for people who are actually at ease with doing the hard work of becoming a very good trader.

This type of person has to be of an analytical nature, and by no means superficial. Being profitable consistently in trading requires hard work. If you expect some type of extraordinary solution that will make you rich overnight with a minimal amount of effort from your part then you will be disappointed. Such a thing does not exist.

If you want to become a top trader you need to work hard and be passionate about trading. The sooner you understand this, the better. You will stop fishing for the magic indicator or some sort of automated program that will do all the trading for you and provide good returns.

Instead, you will begin to concentrate all your efforts on what really matters. Every movement that price makes, interpreting it and putting it together to help you make the best trading decisions possible.

One more thing I would like to add here concerns timeframes. You can use what is presented in this book on any timeframe starting from the five minutes timeframe up. If you prefer a swing trading approach to fit your busy schedule you can use the one hour or four hour charts, if you have more time on your hands to dedicate to trading, you can use the thirty minutes charts or even the fifteen or five minutes zoomed out charts.

I do not recommend trading a timeframe lower than a zoomed out five minutes one because it will expose you to the daily trading noise and random movements to the point where your trading will start to resemble gambling.

WHY SHOULD YOU READ IT?

First of all, let me say that this book will be organized in chapters, each building on the next one. Every concept, technique, trading idea will be thoroughly explained.

The logic behind it, what purpose it serves and how you can benefit from each concept or technique in actual trading will also be explained.

I will use a lot of chart examples, and I do mean a lot, because the best way to learn is to visualize what is being discussed.

As you surely have guessed from the title, this is a book about price action, about price movements, how to interpret them, how to put them together to formulate trading ideas.

The type of trading you will learn by reading this book applies to all financial markets. This is because I do not use any technical indicators whatsoever or some other type of tools that can be suitable for some markets while, at the same time, not applicable in others.

I do not use a sort of market dependent technical analysis technique that can be more efficient in one market and less in another because of market particularities. If you have read something of mine in the past you know that I do not recommend using technical indicators in your trading as they are all constructed on past price action that you can see with your naked eye on the chart.

They are all lagging. The best indicator you can have is your brain analyzing the raw price movements. This doesn't necessarily mean that you cannot make some profits trading with indicators. However, my experience is that these profits will not be consistent. You will win some, you will lose some, you will lose some more, depending on how the market is moving.

If you are not completely new to trading and you have tried out some of the most popular technical indicators you probably know what I mean.

The type of trading that will be discussed is based on the underlying forces that make the price of any particular financial instrument move up or down. That is supply and demand and crowd behavior. The techniques you will learn are based solely on reading the price action on the naked chart in front of you, with the main purpose of discovering what are the buyers and seller doing, and what are they most likely to do next. The price movements on any financial market have one common denominator. Crowd behavior.

This crowd consists of people who buy and people who sell. The selling and buying process is what creates the price movements you see on any chart. The people who buy and sell are called traders but, before being traders, they are people with emotions which always exhibit the same type of predictable behavior when engaging in the processes of buying and selling.

This being said, you can use the methods learned here to trade any electronically traded financial instrument. If that instrument is traded by people like you and me, with all sorts of emotional behavior, it does not matter if it is the Stock market, the Forex market, Futures, Commodities, Indices, Options, Bonds, CFD, ETF and so forth.

It will work just as good in any of these because people's fear or greed makes them act in predictable patterns.

Therefore, one reason to read it, would be that it is about reading and interpreting the price action, thus making it effective in just about any market you want to trade in. Another reason, and perhaps the most important, would be the price action techniques themselves. If you have read about price action trading before you have probably seen discussions about candlesticks, about candlestick wicks that show rejection of a certain price area, about candlestick patterns like "hammer", "morning star", about price patterns, continuation or reversal ones, like "double top", "head and shoulders", "flag" and so on.

Well, this book is nothing like that. I have covered this type of price action techniques to use for reading the markets in some of my other books that I have written in the past. This book will be about core price action concepts and strategies, the type that you will not find very easily elsewhere, if at all. The reason I say this is that all the price action concepts and techniques that you will see in this book are the result of my personal trading experience.

I've read many books on trading over the years, I've watched the markets daily for a long time. As a result of this, I have managed to take some general concepts about trading, modify, test, tweak again as many times as it takes and apply them successfully in trading. It might be that someone, reading the same books as me over the years, might have arrived to roughly the same overall interpretations, and, as a consequence, developed a similar approach to trading. The odds of this are however very slim. You will see why when you actually get into the contents of the book.

HOW WILL READING THIS IMPROVE YOUR TRADING ?

What you will be reading throughout this material is not about just scratching the surface of price action analysis with candlestick patterns and price patterns, like triangles, flags and hammer candlesticks at a support or resistance level.

As I said, I have covered this type of price action in some of my earlier books. This is not to say, that the above approach is not effective. It is actually, but this book will be covering a more in depth, analytical type of price action, which is even more rewarding and reliable if learned and applied correctly. It is about what is generally recognized as pure price action trading.

If learned and used properly you will be able to see the market movements with different eyes, it will give you a clear market structure that will enhance your decision making process. I am not the type of person who will use expressions like "holy grail" so I will refrain from this type of language to describe the trading methods presented in this book. I am going to let you decide of course, how much value this book adds to your trading, after you have read it and put it into practice.

You will be introduced to concepts like fair price areas, value of price, price of control, the shifting of value, supply and demand key levels, market balance and imbalance, responsive and initiative price movements, excess price, finding the trail of the long term traders that move the markets and many more.

You will be introduced to some new price action ideas that will make you see the price movements in a more structured way, you will have a clear understanding of how price behaves and why. I will then go on further to show how you can use this newly found knowledge in your actual trading with logically and carefully explained chart illustrations and commentaries.

I will be moving further on to provide trading ideas and methods of incorporating the new concepts in your day to day trading, in the form of a complete trading plan, that will take you through all the stages of analyzing the market, interpreting it, finding trading setups and executing them.

Okay, I think I am done with the introductions, it might be wise to move on to the actual essence of the book, which is the price action you will be learning.

CHAPTER TWO - FAIR VALUE OF PRICE

Let me just say briefly that the price action concepts and ideas that you will find in this material are somewhat inspired, to an extent, from the market profile technique of analyzing the markets. I say to an extent because it will go on to diverge quite a bit from the market profile way of studying the markets.

Over the years I did quite a bit of research on this way of market studying but I never did actually trade the markets using market profile. My impression was that it provided solid ideas to build on but it lacked practicality. What I did was to take part of what I thought were solid concepts, added some of my own, and used them as a solid base ground to build on. The final outcome that you will read in this book has actually very little to do with how market profile technique does with analyzing the markets.

The markets, at their essence, were built to facilitate trading. The price action movements on any chart on your trading platform are the result of this primary objective of the market. Simply put, what you see on your charts is the result of supply and demand principle. Otherwise said, if demand exceeds supply, the total trading volume of buyers is greater than the total trading volume of sellers, causing the price of any particular financial instrument to go up.

Conversely, if supply exceeds demand, the total trading volume of sellers overcomes that of the buyer's, causing the price to fall down. In the scenario where supply equals demand the price will not move in any direction, instead it will begin to accumulate or consolidate, and develop what I call a fair value of price, or an area where both buyers and sellers agree that the instrument or security is correctly priced considering the underlying fundamentals.

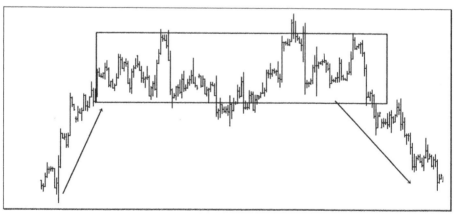

FIGURE 1: MARKET PHASES USED FOR TRADING FACILITATION

Do not worry, as there will be plenty of full charts later on throughout the book when we discuss how to take advantage of what is presented, in actual trading. The charts will have the name of the financial instrument in cause, along with the price and time axes.

At this early stage in the chapter though, as I am just beginning to explain how to recognize the market structure and the fair value concept, I will use charts like the above one without any other irrelevant information.

The above chart illustrates how supply and demand translates into price movements. The first upwards move at the beginning of the chart, accompanied by that up arrow, is the result of demand exceeding supply for this security. To put it in practical terms, the total volume of buy orders was greater than the total volume of sell orders, which is causing the price to move up.

Regardless of their reasons, the sellers did not have the confidence to enter into the market at that time. They probably felt that the price of this security is not in accordance with their evaluation of the latest fundamental news and it should be priced higher. Only then they will enter the market, creating a supply. And they did that in the area marked with a rectangle. They entered the market increasing supply and causing the price to stop its ascent, as a result. This area where the price is moving sideways, shows that the market has found a balance, the supply is matching demand.

The market has met its purpose to facilitate trading between buyers and sellers. At this point, both buyers and sellers are in accordance that this price area is fair for this security and neither is interested in stepping into the market to push the price higher or lower. They feel content with keeping the price in that confined area, with the buyers stepping in only as much as it takes to keep the price from falling below the lower boundary of this area, and the sellers entering at the higher boundary of the area, to push the price back inside.

It is important for you to understand the following: the buyers and sellers that I speak of and that behave in this manner are not individuals like you and me. In any given market, there are two types of traders, short term traders and long term traders. The short term traders are mainly retail individual traders like you, me and many others. Short term traders like us engage in trading with one thing in mind. To speculate the market. We make trading decisions based on the short term timeframes, we do not really care about the weekly or the monthly trend. We do not make trading decisions based on the underlying fundamentals of a stock or foreign exchange pair.

Some of us read the news, avoid trading when important news come out, some even try to trade the news. We use the news in a speculative way, we avoid trading when they are released but, I think it is safe to say that the impact fundamental news has on our trading stops here. We do not make trading decisions based on the news. The only thing we are really interested in is turn a profit from speculating market imbalance. And we do this by analyzing the market from a technical point of view, in the hope of finding a solid trading opportunity. We wait patiently for the opportunity to present itself, we act on it to make a small profit hopefully, exit and repeat the process.

Why should we care much about the overall health of one market or another? We do not keep open positions for a year, it doesn't matter to small individual traders like you and me that the Euro currency might collapse in three months for example. So what? It doesn't affect my trading at all you would say. I don't have any long term investments in the Euro. I don't care if the Euro falls or not, I will not be affected directly in any way. My job is to take advantage of the market movements that this fall will generate. I will be trading the EURUSD in and out as many times as I can without giving it a single thought to the euro's overall health compared to the other currencies and all the economic implications that will result from this.

And then there is the long term trader. And he does care about the euro's health. He has open long term positions on the euro. He, this long term trader, is actually an investment fund with large amounts of capital at his disposal. He is looking to invest on a long term basis as he sees fit, in order to keep the capital growing bit by bit each month, to keep his clients satisfied.

He operates with large trading volumes, as opposed to you and me. He will suffer direct losses if the euro falls, so he decides to sell the euros and close his open positions. He will maybe decide to take that capital and invest it in gold until the market becomes more stable. When the uncertainty returns to a normal level he will close all or part of his gold positions and buy the euro again, at a much lower price this time. The long term traders are the banks and all the other large financial institutions. These are the ones that move the market due to their large trading volumes. They do analyze the markets from a fundamental point of view and they adjust their open positions based on this analysis, they distribute their investment capital in a way that will minimize risk and maximize returns.

They are very interested in the overall status of the market because they are in the front line, their capital is exposed to risk, they will suffer direct loses if they do not have a bird's eye view of the market at all times. This is why they usually keep to the higher timeframes, to see the big picture.

Having read all of the above regarding short term and long term traders, looking at the first chart, what type of behavior do you observe there? It's the long term traders who have the power to move the price up or down, and it's the long term traders who decide to keep the price confined into a sideways motion. They are the ones with the huge trading volumes, and the trading volume is what moves the market. You and me, we do not have any impact on the price movements whatsoever.

Making the connection with the price movements on the chart above, the long term traders decided that the price should be higher at the beginning of the chart on the left. The long term buyer entered the market creating demand while the long term seller stayed on the sidelines. He will enter the market to sell at a more advantageous price for him. Why should the seller make his appearance earlier? He has read the same news as the buyer and he made the same fundamental analysis.

Both long term buyer and seller agree that the price should be higher. This type of behavior is what generates the price movements you see on your charts. Throughout this book, whenever I will discuss about buyer and seller behavior, you will now be aware that I am talking about the long term traders. They are the ones who move the markets, it makes all the sense in the world to study their behavior, observe how price moves as a result of their actions, and formulate concepts, rules and strategies to follow what they do, to be in the same boat as them.

We have to discover their footsteps and follow them. This is the main idea behind the price action concepts and strategies I will be presenting throughout this book.

With respect to this chapter, we are especially interested in price movements like that in the above chart, emphasized by the rectangle, because this is where fair value of price is born. You will see shortly what exactly fair value is, how to correctly mark it, and how much insight it can provide when making trading decisions. Back to the chart above, after price has moved sideways for quite a while, it finally breaks to the downside.

This is shown on the chart by the down arrow that accompanies the down move of price on the right of the chart. Supply has exceeded demand causing the market to move down, seeking buyers so that it can again facilitate trading between both parties. Price will go down until demand will be met or, in other words, until it sparks buying interest, which will result in increase of buying orders for the security.

WHAT IS THE FAIR VALUE AREA?

As you may have guessed from my comments above, the fair value of any given forex pair, stock or commodity is an area where price has spent most time trading at, an area where supply met demand and buyers and sellers both, agreed that this price area corresponds to their current expectations. They are happy leaving the price at the current level, they consider it a fair price at this moment. They say pictures are better than a thousand words and I cannot disagree.

Therefore, building on the first chart, let us see where the fair value area is exactly.

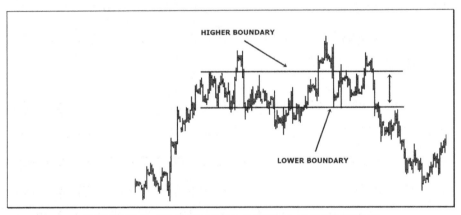

FIGURE 2: FAIR VALUE AREA BOUNDARIES

The price area confined between those two horizontal lines in the chart above is the fair value area. From this point on, as I will discuss a lot about the fair value areas, I will simplify the label and refer to them as "value areas" or "value" It is not important how you call them, as long as you get used to identifying them and recognize their true meaning and importance when trading.

Why did I choose the value boundaries that way?

You can see that price has gone three times above the higher limit of value that I have drawn on the chart and two times below the lower limit. However, price did not spend much time in those areas, it just tested those levels, found demand on the downside, supply on the upside and quickly retraced back in the area where the bulk of trading was taking place. These areas where price deviates away from value for a short period of time only to come back inside it is what I call excess price. We will be discussing more in detail about these areas shortly.

As I state at the beginning of the book, this type of trading is highly discretionary. It will take some practice from your part to learn how to identify correctly the value areas on your charts. Do not worry though, it is not hard, all it takes is some screen time and you will be able to see and mark them very easily. The one thing to remember when marking the boundaries of value is that this is not something that you have to measure precisely. Do not think of those upper and lower value limits as exact lines on the chart. Think of them as price areas or price zones. They do not even have to be lines, you can draw a rectangle to engulf the value area if it helps more. This is not supposed to be approached with mathematical precision. When you look for the value, look carefully at the price movements in question and notice the area where the vast majority of trading took place.

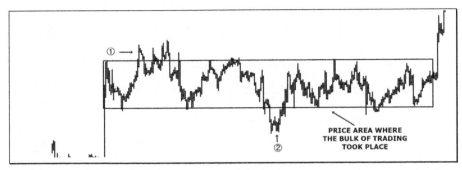

FIGURE 3: THE BULK OF TRADING DEFINES THE VALUE AREA

Notice the chart above. If we were to exclude time out of the equation and plot just the price on our chart, you would not see any blank, white space. You would see price cramped into a small area. In this situation the price area marked with a rectangle above would look like a big bulge because there is much trading activity there. Think of this as eliminating all the blank space between the price movements that are inside the value area. What you will get is a bulge of price on the left of the chart. The price zones that I have market with "1" and "2" would be very skinny because there is not much trading going on in those areas. Notice the price movements inside the value area included in the rectangle above. They populate the same price area over and over again. Price is rotating up and down.

This is what creates the value of price. Both buyers and sellers acknowledge this price area to be fair at this moment in time for this security.

They feel comfortable leaving it in this area until further fundamental developments will change the status quo.

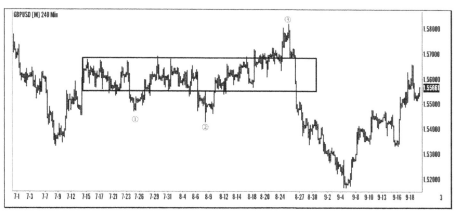

FIGURE 4: VALUE AREA EXAMPLE

See another example of value developed on the GBPUSD chart. Notice where I choose to draw the value area limits. When identifying and marking the value area boundaries, try to leave out as much blank space as you possibly can, above and below. Notice the price movements below the value area marked as "1" and "2". There are huge gaps to the left and to the right of both of them. Price did not spent much time in these price areas. The same with the "3" price move above value.

All three are excess price. The consensus between long term buyers and sellers is what gives value to a certain price area. On these three small moves below and above the value area there is no consensus. On "1" and "2", buyers step into the market and push the price back into where the bulk of trading is taking place. Right inside the rectangle. On "3", the sellers step into the market to push the price lower into the recognized value.

This is how they operate. They want to buy below and sell above what they consider a fair price. Price going higher, above the perceived value, is considered a selling opportunity by the long term seller and price going lower, below what is generally accepted as the fair value of this currency pair, is looked upon as a buying opportunity by the long term buyer.

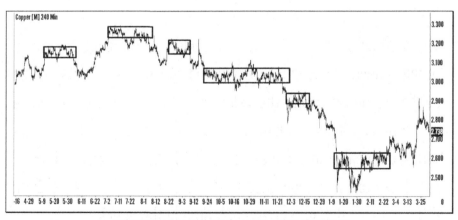

FIGURE 5: VALUE AREA EXAMPLES

See the above example. Every chart looks the same way. Price moves from value area to another value area. The market fulfills its role to facilitate trading between buyers and sellers. When supply exceeds demand, price goes lower to find equilibrium between buyers and sellers, creating value of price. The process in repeated over and over until the situation changes and buyers become dominant at the end of the chart there. Observe also the different sizes of each value area of price. As with other concepts in trading, the bigger the value area, the more significant it is. We will discuss more about this later.

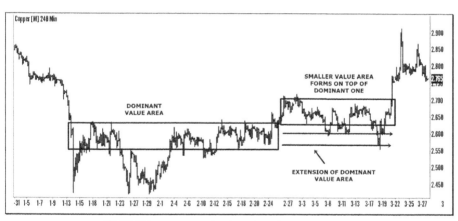

FIGURE 6: VALUE ON TOP OF VALUE

Value can develop on top of other value area. In the above chart, the bigger rectangle is the big value area in that price region. The two long horizontal arrows to the right side of it represent the territory of this dominant value area. We will observe later just how territorial these value areas can become. You can see price starting to go above the value area in what seems at first to be excess price. In order for that to be validated as excess, as explained in the above charts and comments, price would have had to spend a limited amount of time in that area, only to move back down inside the value area.

Instead, price does not go back inside value, it starts to populate that space with small up and down movements. The upper limit of the dominant value area acts as a support level for price. A new, smaller value area, is formed above what was recognized as value. We will get into all this and much more, later throughout the book when I will be discussing about the shifting of value concept. For now we will concentrate on recognizing value areas on charts.

FIGURE 7: VALUE AREA TAKING SHAPE BELOW DOMINANT VALUE

Conversely, small value develops outside, below the dominant value area. The lower limit of the big value area is acting as resistance for price. There was not enough demand at the lower limit of the value area to push price back up inside and form excess price. Instead, price remains below the value area, making small up and down, rotating movements, to give this area of price value. I am talking about the smaller rectangle in the chart above, below the value. Eventually, price finds enough demand to go back inside the bigger value area's territory.

Interestingly enough, it travels straight to the dominant value area's higher boundary, find very strong supply of selling orders there, resulting in a strong downwards move. You will find this type of price movements a lot on your charts. We will discuss more in detail about how value areas interact with each other and how we can take advantage of this fact later on.

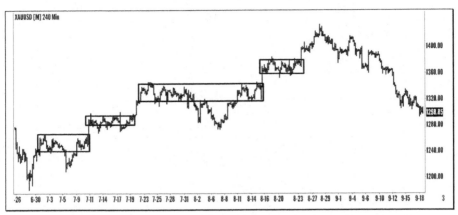

FIGURE 8: PRICE GOING UP FROM ONE VALUE AREA TO ANOTHER

Please note yet another example of how the market's auction process develops value. All those rectangles on the chart are value areas. Some smaller, some bigger, they all give the price area value.

The market moves from balance to imbalance, between supply and demand. When in value, the market is balanced, meaning that supply is roughly the same as demand and buyers and sellers are content executing trading in that area. When the market is not in value, it is actually seeking value by moving higher and higher. This is the market phase where demand exceeds supply causing the market to move up until it finds sellers.

This is part of the market structure. You will have a complete understanding of it when we discuss about how value moves.

> BEFORE WE GO FURTHER, PLEASE STOP READING AND OPEN UP YOUR TRADING PLATFORM. OPEN A CHART, SCROLL BACK FOR A PERIOD OF TIME AT YOUR CHOOSING AND IDENTIFY THE VALUE AREAS ON THAT CHART ONE BY ONE. THIS CAN BE LEARNED BEST BY PRACTICE. DO THIS UNTIL IT BECOMES EASY FOR YOU TO SPOT VALUE AREAS WITH A SIMPLE GLIMPSE. IT SHOULDN'T TAKE LONG AT ALL.

GUIDELINES

- OBSERVE THE AREAS WHERE PRICE HAS BEEN TRADING THE MOST
- OBSERVE THE AREAS ABOVE AND BELOW, WHERE PRICE HAS BEEN TRADING THE LEAST. THAT IS EXCESS
- SEEK TO LEAVE OUT AS MUCH BLANK SPACE AS POSSIBLE IN ORDER TO CORRECTLY SEPARATE VALUE FROM EXCESS PRICE.
- REPETITIVE UP AND DOWN MOVEMENTS IN THE SAME PRICE AREA IS WHAT CREATES VALUE.
- IMAGINE THAT THE HORIZONTAL TIME AXIS ON YOUR CHART DISAPPEARS. THE BLANK SPACE IN BETWEEN PRICE MOVEMENTS DOES NOT EXIST ANYMORE. THESE MOVEMENTS WILL CREATE A BULGE OR SWELLING. THIS BULGE IS THE VALUE AREA. ON THE UPPER SIDE AND LOWER SIDE OF THE SWELLING, WHERE PRICE TRADED THE LEAST, THERE WILL BE ALMOST FLAT TERRITORY. THAT IS THE EXCESS PRICE.
- AFTER MARKING THE VALUE AREAS ON YOUR CHART AND GETTING USED TO SPOTTING THEM, EXTEND THEM ONE BY ONE TO THE RIGHT SIDE OF THE CHART AND SEE HOW FUTURE PRICE MOVEMENTS REACT WHEN THEY COME INTO CONTACT WITH THE EACH VALUE BOUNDARY.

TRADING VOLUME

The trading volume is basically the total number of shares traded on the stock market, the total number of futures contracts traded in the futures market or the total number of full lots traded in the forex market. The forex market has no centralized exchange actually so it is difficult to know exactly how many transactions were made. Volume can be estimated in a number of ways though. Volume is used to identify support and resistance levels in the market, to gauge the strength of price movements, but it is best used in conjunction with other concepts and methods of analyzing the price. The identifying of value areas as described above is highly successful in discovering where the volume concentration of a financial instrument lies.

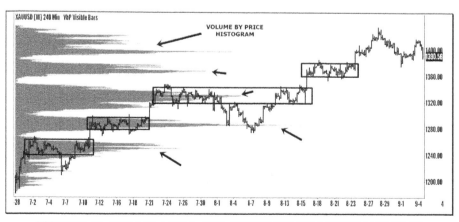

FIGURE 9: VALUE AREA RELATION TO TRADING VOLUME

What you see here is the same exact chart as the last one above with the value areas in rising price. I have added a volume by price histogram on the left side of the chart. What this does is plot the trading volume of this financial pair but with respect to price not to time. It shows volume of trading at price levels. I am not going to use this histogram in actual trading. I've added it so you can grasp the true significance of value areas. I have explained the underlying supply and demand process and the long term versus short term trader behavior for you to realize the importance of the value of price.

Volume by price goes further to show you that learning to spot value of price on your charts is going to improve your trading significantly. Those big spikes on the horizontal histogram on the left signify big trading volume. The longer the histogram extends to the right side of the chart, the higher the trading volume is at that particular price. Notice where the value areas are on the chart as we have identified them earlier and look at the spikes of volume in that histogram.

The highest volume is at the same price level as our value areas. See how the volume spikes pierce every value area. In markets like the foreign exchange, where there is no centralized real volume available, you can see very clearly by marking the value areas on the charts, where the bulk of trading volume is.

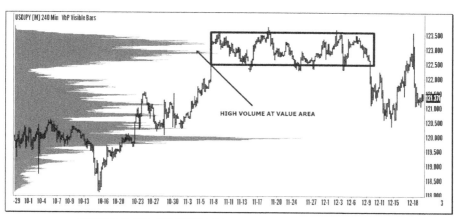

FIGURE 10: FOREX VOLUME AT VALUE AREA

Just as with the first chart, see above the USDJPY forex pair. Notice how the value area shows the high volume price areas. This goes to show you that the naked chart is all you need for trading. Marking the value of price on your charts will do much more than showing the bulk of trading volume. The volume is plotted this way to help identify areas of support and resistance as I said before. So, this is one role that the value areas will have in your trading but certainly not the only one.

EXCESS PRICE

The excess price you have seen in the above examples, that takes shape above or below a value area, we can interpret as follows.

- IT SHOWS THE FOOTPRINT OF THE LONG TERM TRADER AND HIS INTENTIONS
- THE EXCESS REVEALS CLEAR SUPPLY AND DEMAND ZONES
- AS A RESULT, THEY WILL SERVE AS STRONG SUPPORT OR RESISTANCE LEVELS. IT SHOWS REJECTION OF A PRICE LEVEL

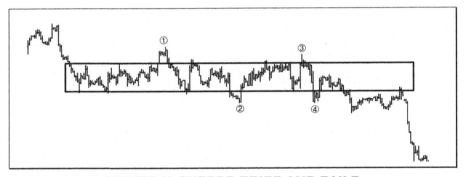

FIGURE 11: EXCESS PRICE AND TAILS

Observe how price behaves at the "1" area. It goes outside of what is perceived as value for price but it spends very little time there. It comes back down again to making rotating up and down moves which will consolidate the value area even more. The same thing happens at "2" and "4" area levels. This reveals the buyers and the sellers clearly entering the market as they consider these levels of price as advantageous for them.

Remember that the long term traders, or smart money, or big institutions, whatever you want to call them, have a different, bigger perspective on the market than you and me. What they consider an advantageous price for entering the market in either direction, might not be perceived by us, the short term traders, as advantageous.

This is because we look at different things than the long term traders. We keep to the shorter timeframes, we base our trading decisions on shorter term price action than the institutional traders do. Maybe, in area "1" on the above chart, the long term trader with the overall picture of the market in front of him, has seen on the daily timeframe that price is touching the lower limit of a big value area in the daily chart.

He sees this as an advantageous price level to sell so he steps in. We can't see that lower limit of value on the daily chart because we are focusing on this chart above, which shows price on the four hours timeframe. Maybe, according to your set of rules of analyzing the market, this "1" area is not good enough for selling into it, but you can see that the long term trader has a different opinion than you. His opinion counts.

He has the trading money which can push the price in one direction or another. You and me, we do not. But we do have the capability to spy on the long term trader and observe what he does, so we can be on the same side as him. Excess price is a very strong way of seeing this long term trader entering the market. On point "3" in the above chart we have what is called a tail. It has all the characteristics and underlying implications of the excess price, but is stronger.

Please remember this. The less time price spends at a certain price level, the more effective that price level will be in providing support or resistance for future price action. Why? Because less time spent shows greater rejection. At "1", "2" and "4" excess zones you can see price going outside value, printing five to ten bars of price in these areas and returning inside value. This shows rejection of these price areas.

Otherwise said, the market has found supply at "1" and demand at "2" and "4". Expressed even more simple than this, there were selling orders at "1" price area, that increased the supply causing the price to go back inside value. Conversely, there were buying orders at "2" and "4" price zones that increased the demand of this security, causing the price to get right back inside value. Point "3" on the chart above, has the same meaning, but enhanced, stronger.

Observe how price goes above value and spends there the least amount of time possible. This level is rejected very swiftly. The supply increased rapidly here. This is a clearer footprint of sellers entering the market. This is excess price also, but because of the way it looks, it is often referred to as a tail or even a spike. It doesn't matter how you call it. The important thing is to grasp its meaning when you see it on the chart.

To prove the point even further, consider this. In the above chart, you have four excess zones, two above and two below value. The tail, which is greater sign of rejection is on the upside of value. Below value, we have only two normal excess price zones. At this point, after "4" excess zone has completed and price has gone back inside value, we should be inclined to think that price will break the value on the downside and continue further down. That is what happened, price broke value to the downside, made a small value area there, showing rejection of the bigger value's lower limit, touched the lower boundary of the value area to test it. It found supply or selling orders there that caused the price to move further down, away from the value area.

Why would we have been inclined to think this is going to happen before it actually happened? One of the reasons that would inoculate this assumption is the point "3" tail above the value area. The other reasons will be discussed in upcoming chapters. The tail shows greater rejection of that price area.

On the downside of value we do not have any tails. We can then make the supposition that sellers are stronger or that supply is slightly greater than demand because sellers are more motivated to push the price back to value than the buyers are pushing it back up inside value.

Of course, we need more than a simple tail to judge if price is going to go up or down from a certain point. But recognizing this excess price in the market will definitely provide more insight when it comes to making trading decisions.

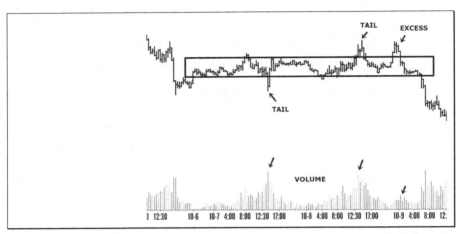

FIGURE 12: EXCESS AND TAILS RELATION TO TRADING VOLUME

The example above show tails developing both above and below value. The addition of one more excess price area above value is adding to the possibility that the sellers will eventually win the battle with buyers and push the price below, away from the value area.

Observe that the tail below value is showing a bigger rejection of price in that area, as price only stays there for two bars. The tail above value comes late, price prints four bars in that area. However, it is a strong rejection nevertheless.

See the one bar in the middle that protrudes away from its surrounding price bars. That is the tail. You do not have to count price bars to quantify how much rejection of price one movement is showing. It is just my way of explaining what is happening.

Generally, if you see a price spike like the tail below value in the above chart, you should regard it as a footprint of buyers or demand present at that level of price. Just remember that the less time price is spending in that price area, the bigger the rejection of the same price area is.

Look at the volume spikes for each excess price or tail. Again, this clearly shows buyers and sellers entering the market. The trading volume of the excess price zone above value seems little because the move happened in a time interval where the trading activity is usually smaller compared to the rest of the day.

However, that too shows a bulge in volume when compared to surrounding trading volume in that time period.

> PLEASE STOP READING AT THIS POINT. GO TO YOUR CHARTS AGAIN WHERE YOU HAVE DONE PRACTICE TO DISCOVER VALUE AREAS AND NOTICE THE CORRESPONDING EXCESS PRICE AND TAILS FOR EACH. APPLY THE TYPE OF THINKING DESCRIBED ABOVE AND SEE IF YOU COME TO ROUGHLY THE SAME CONCLUSIONS AS I DID. SEE WHAT EXCESS AND TAILS THERE ARE BELOW AND ABOVE THE VALUE AREA AND WHAT DOES PRICE DO AFTER THE EXCESS IS SHOWN. WHAT IS THE RELATION BETWEEN THE EXCESS AND THE SUBSEQUENT BREAK OF THE VALUE TO THE UP OR DOWNSIDE? DRAW YOUR OWN CONCLUSIONS.

CONTROL PRICE

You have seen how the market gives value to certain price areas. It starts rotating up and down in a sideways motion. These up and down movements inside the value area, in their way from one value area limit to another and back, go through a price level where the market has been showing the greatest trading activity. That price level is the control price. It is basically a pivotal support and resistance level inside the value area.

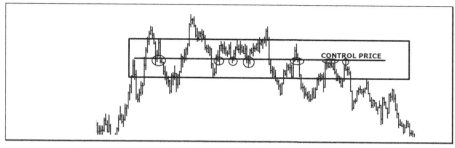

FIGURE 13: CONTROL PRICE OF VALUE AREA

Observe the horizontal line inside the value area. That is roughly the price level in the value area where price has spent the greatest amount of time. See the little circles that capture each time price has gone to this level, retraced, touched it again and developed tiny value areas just above and below it. This is the control price of this value area. It controls the up and down movements inside it. Nearly every up or down move in the value area, stops at this control price line, rejects it for a little while and develops small value with that sideways trading above and below it.

This is nothing more than a pivotal support and resistance level for price as I said before. It is called pivotal because how price oscillates around it. It is both a support and a resistance for price. A support for price approaching it from the value area high and a resistance for price approaching it from the value area low. If value of price is where the majority of trading activity and volume takes place, the control price is a price level inside the value with the highest trading activity and volume from that value area.

The best way to think of this control price is to imagine it as having gravity. It is attracting price inside the value area to it. It is exerting gravitational pull on all price inside the value area. As long as price stays in the value area it will be attracted by this control price and it will spend more time at and around it than anywhere else in the value area.

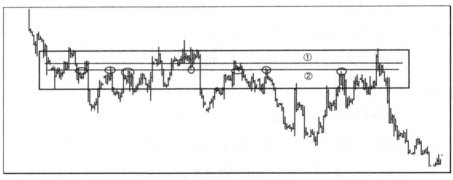

FIGURE 14: APPARENT MULTIPLE CONTROL AREAS

Observe the value area above. In situations like these where the value area is very big in size, over time, it will start to develop inside it more than one pivotal support and resistance level. At a first glance, it will be difficult to spot which of those levels is actually the control price or which has the most trading activity around it. See this example above. Both of those two lines inside the value area have trading activity around them, price seems to be taking turns in gravitating each.

You need to look carefully and find the one which price has interacted the most with. In the chart above, the control price of the value area is line "2" that is situated more to the middle of the value area. You can see that price made more swings or turning points around this price level than around the one above it labeled as "1". Also, there are more small value areas around the "2" line.

In situations where it becomes very hard to decide which support and resistance level has the greatest control over price inside the value area, always choose the one which is located closer to the middle of the value area. The control price in the above chart, besides controlling price better than the "1" line, is also the one closer to the middle of the value area.

There will be situations where the value areas are smaller in size than that in the chart above. Being smaller, it will automatically not have the same amount of rotating up and down moves between its boundaries. In such value areas, you will find it difficult to see the control price. This doesn't mean that there is no control price. There is, there always is one. You just can't see it from the timeframe you are looking at.

Mark your value area on the timeframe you are interested in

trading on and move down to a lower timeframe to see and mark the control price. It will be there. The up and down moves inside the value area and the tiny sideways motions that price makes around a certain level will be easier to spot on the lower timeframe.

> I AM GOING TO ASK YOU NOW, ONCE AGAIN, TO STOP READING AND GO YOUR CHARTS WHERE YOU PREVIOUSLY DID YOUR PRACTICE WITH VALUE AREAS AND EXCESS PRICE. ON THOSE SAME VALUE AREAS, TRY TO FIND THE CONTROL PRICE FOR EACH. FIND OUT WHERE THE GRAVITATIONAL PULL THAT ATTRACTS ALL PRICE IN THE VALUE AREA IS. LOOK FOR SMALL TURNING POINTS AND SMALL VALUE AREAS OR SIDEWAYS MOTION AT OR AROUND ONE PARTICULAR PRICE LEVEL.

If there is more than one and it's hard to find the one with the most gravitational pull on price, move to a slightly lower timeframe. If you still don't see any real difference, choose the one closest to the middle of the value area. Do the same if you cannot see any visible control price on the timeframe you are looking at. If this seems hard, do not worry. There will be more examples discussed throughout the book.

INITIATIVE AND RESPONSIVE TRADING

Earlier, when we discussed about value of price and what the underlying concepts behind it are in terms of supply and demand, I mentioned that both buyers and sellers acknowledge a certain price area to be fair value at that specific moment in time.

As a result, they feel content with keeping the security in the value area, limiting their behavior to selling when price goes above and buying when price goes below value. That is responsive trading activity. There is a balance between supply and demand in the market. But what happens when the buyers or the sellers decide that the current price the security is trading at is not fair anymore? They enter the market, they take the initiative and move price away from value. That is initiative trading activity.

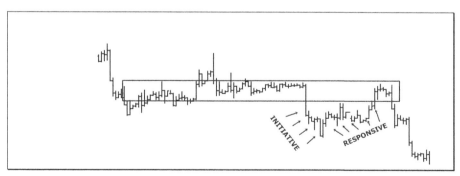

FIGURE 15: INITIATIVE AND RESPONSIVE PRICE MOVEMENTS

Note in the above chart how swiftly price brakes the value to the downside. It only takes a single, huge price bar to move from the upper limit of the value area down, way below the lower boundary of value. This is initiative trading behavior. The sellers feel that this area of price is not as fair anymore, considering the underlying fundamentals they keep track of, and decide to step into the market to push the price down. They do this with force, accompanied by good trading volume.

One way to use the value area in trading, as you will find out later throughout the book is to take advantage of the fact that it attracts price. Therefore, an initiative move away from value area will always need good trading volume in order to be successful. When you see swift, forceful moves like that, away from value, you can be sure that there is good trading volume behind it. The responsive moves however, are different. They do not have the force of the initiative movements. As noted in the above chart, the response of buyers that comes after the sellers taking initiative and pushing price below value fast, is weak. It takes price a long time and some sideways movements to travel its way back inside value, only to find supply once again and give the sellers the possibility to sell at what they consider an advantageous price near the value area high there.

They take the initiative once again and push price back down, even more than the first time. The market is not in balance any more. The sellers are in control.

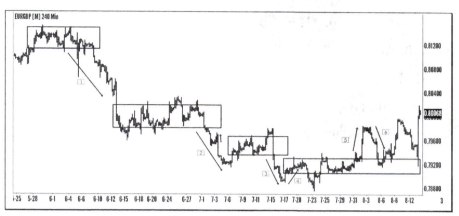

FIGURE 16: MARKET MOVES FROM VALUE TO VALUE WITH INITIATING AND RESPONSIVE MOVES

Note how price moves on this forex pair. It travels from one value area to another with the help of initiative selling. "1", "2", "3", "5" price movements are all initiative movements because they push price away from fair value, regardless of direction. The "5" movement differs from the earlier initiative movements due to the fact that it changes the supply and demand dynamic. If on the first three, the seller shows that he is clearly in charge of this pair by pushing the price down, away from value, on "5", it's the buyer who takes the initiative and starts to push the price back up, away from value. The short term downtrend on this pair might terminate because the dynamic between buyer and seller seems to have changed.

Price exhibited initiative selling until this point, now it shows initiative buying. The "6" move down towards value is responsive selling. As you can see, the initiative selling behavior that took place throughout the chart, did not met any meaningful responsive buying to at least try and push the price back up to value. Only initiative selling movement "3" has a feeble attempt of responsive buying, marked by the "4" price move. The fact that the other initiative selling did not encounter response from buyers, shows that the sellers had complete control at the time. The demand only increased at the bottom of the chart in the last value area. You can see there the buyers making a long tail below that value area which is clear indication of them showing buying interest at this low price level.

The supposition is confirmed when they actually take the initiative and push price away from value on "5". In fact, on the first two initiative selling moves, we did not see any responsive buying. Initiative selling "3" move is where the responsive buying starts.

This too shows that the buyers are starting to take interest in these low prices. The lower the price will go, the greater the demand will increase. More on this type of analysis in the second chapter.

> FOR NOW, PLEASE GO TO YOUR CHARTS AGAIN, MARK THE INITIATIVE AND RESPONSIVE PRICE MOVEMENTS, AND SEE IF YOU CAN MAKE A LINK BETWEEN THEM AND HOW PRICE CHANGES ITS DIRECTION, USING SIMILAR JUDGMENT LIKE THE ONE DESCRIBED ABOVE. DON'T WORRY IF YOU DO NOT. IT IS NOT ALWAYS THIS CLEAR LIKE IN THE EXAMPLE ABOVE.

This is the end of the second chapter. On the next one we will discuss the dynamics of value area shifting or moving directionally and its implications. After practice is done, if you are left with a feeling that you did not completely understand something described in this chapter do not worry, what was presented above will make its way throughout the book in many other examples and explanations. You will get tired of them.

After a while though, I can assure you that you will be very glad you took the time to learn them. They will change the way you trade, the way you analyze the markets. You will become much more confident when trading as you will now have a clear understanding of market structure, your technical analysis approach will be very versatile and very lucrative.

Did you notice that I tend to speak more in terms of supply and demand than in terms of price bars or price moves? This is intentional. The goal is for you to learn and make judgment calls based on the underlying concepts.

The price movements on the charts are just an intermediary between us and supply and demand. We read the price on the chart to find out what is going on behind them. You have to do this type of judgment in the back of your head when you are looking at the charts. You will see by the end of the book the complete thought process that you have to make when you analyze the market. I know that the temptation to just memorize mechanically a set of rules is great, please resist it.

Do not take only a set of rules and chart lines from what is presented above.

Take the thought process. You will become a versatile trader and it will help you to adapt easily to anything the market is throwing at you.

CHAPTER THREE - VALUE SHIFTING

MOVING VALUE

Up to this point I have been describing the value of price as the area where the market has spent the most time trading at.

The area where supply meets demand and, as a consequence, price moves sideways, rotating up and down, between supply at value area high and demand at value area low. However, I did say that it is also where the bulk of trading volume takes place. The price movements can give value to a financial security even if the supply and demand are not in complete balance. If there is a slight imbalance, let's say that supply is slightly bigger than demand, how will the price movements look like?

Well, that would mean the market is bearish and that the sellers are slowly pushing the price down. Slowly being the key word.

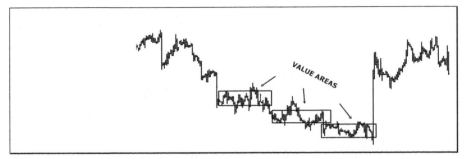

FIGURE 17: PRICE MOVING SLOWLY IN A DOWN DIRECTION

Notice the price action in the above chart. See those three value areas. Watch how close they are to one another. They practically merge into one single value area with a bearish bias. You can hardly tell where one ends and the other one begins. Actually you can, because you can see price behavior around each value boundary low, but there is some difficulty in trying to separate them. Each value area low is acting as resistance for the next value's high. The point I am trying to make is that the value areas are practically joined together.

The value slowly extends downwards. There is no swift price move downwards in between them like the one just above the first value area for example. There is a slight imbalance in supply and demand, favoring the sellers, but the imbalance is small, otherwise the price will fall down with force and not exhibit this type of small shifting movement to the downside. As I said earlier, we need to think of the underlying forces of supply and demand more than concentrating on the lines we draw on our chart.

Remember about the bulk of trading volume and its relation to value of price. What do you think the volume by price histogram will show if plotted on this chart? It will show no gaps of volume between the three value areas. That is because they are very close, each one builds on the previous. Let's see the same chart again.

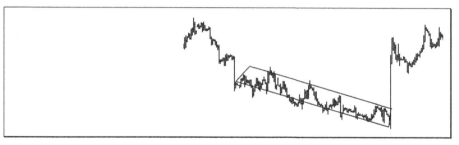

FIGURE 18: SHIFTING VALUE OF PRICE

Can we consider this whole area a single value of price? Yes we can. It has the same underlying characteristics as any of those depicted in the first chapter. It contains the bulk of trading volume, it has a value high, a value low, some excess price zones and a control price, which I did not mark. We will discuss about it shortly. It also has rotations or up and down movements that travel from the value area high to value area low and back.

Of course, with the sellers being in control and pushing the price down slowly, we do not get to have all the price rotations at the same price level over and over again as it happens in value areas where price is moving completely sideways due to perfect balance between supply and demand. Those type of value areas will offer extremely powerful support and resistance areas for future price action. In the case of the shifting value areas, price spends less time at one single price area.

However, we will use these value areas to construct a bigger price structure that will give us the same power as those described in the first chapter. Have a little patience, it will soon start to get interesting.

FIGURE 19: SHIFTING VALUE AREAS

Can we join the "2" and "3" small value areas in the above chart to form a single shifting value area like I did with "1" and "4"?. No. Look at the "1" value area and then look at the "4" value area. They are very similar. The demand is slightly greater than supply is. The result of this is that price is being pushed upwards slowly. The price is making up and down rotations with each going only a bit higher than the previous.

You can see the rotations of price inside the value areas marked with those up and down arrows. This produces the value area high and value area low limits as emphasized by the rectangular shapes. The market is populating roughly the same area of price, as there is no strong move upwards. This gives the possibility to join any number of small value areas that develop just above or below the previous value, into a single, bigger shifting value area.

Why can't we join the "2" and "3" small value areas to form a bigger down shifting value area? Because of the initiative move down, away from value "2". That is the big strong down move in between "2" and "3". The imbalance between supply and demand is significant there.

The sellers are in complete control, they do not feel that the "2" price area is fair for this security and they push price down with force. The price then develops value "3". They are two distinct value areas that cannot be treated as one because of that big down move between them. In the "1" and "4" shifting value areas these is no sight of such a strong move in one direction or another. The imbalance of supply and demand is slightly favoring the buyers who manage to push price only a little bit higher with each rotation.

> IT'S TIME FOR SOME PRACTICE AGAIN. TRY TO GET FAMILIAR WITH HOW VALUE MOVES. ANALYZE THE CHARTS AND MARK THEM AS YOU DID WITH THE HORIZONTAL VALUE AREAS. SEEK RELATIVELY TIGHT AREAS WHERE PRICE HAS MADE SMALL VALUE NEXT TO ANOTHER SMALL VALUE REPEATEDLY. THIS AREA SHOULD LOOK LIKE A UNITARY BLOCK OF PRICE ACTIVITY, WITHOUT STRONG MOVES SEPARATING THE VALUE AREAS. AS WITH HORIZONTAL VALUE, THERE IS NO NEED TO BE EXTREMELY PRECISE. JUST TRY TO ENGULF THE AREA WHERE YOU SEE THAT THE BULK OF TRADING TOOK PLACE. PAY ATTENTION TO THE EXCESS PRICE ALSO.

CONSTRUCTING THE BIG PICTURE

Have you ever had the curiosity to look at a monthly chart of any financial instrument? I want you to turn your attention for a minute on such a chart. Scrolling through these charts will have you realize quickly that the current price activity is taking place, in the majority of situations, inside a bigger value area on the monthly or even weekly chart of the same security.

There is always a value area present, it all depends on your perspective on the market. It depends on the timeframe you use for trading. We are going to use the value areas presented above and in the first chapter to construct the bigger value.

FIGURE 20: VALUE MOVES UP

See the value areas that price makes on its way up. The "2" value area is a shifting value like those described just above. The other ones have developed in a balance between supply and demand causing the price to move sideways. These are the ones described in the first chapter.

Remember when I presented the control price of value area, I said to notice how price makes small sideways movements above and below it.

I want you to think of the value areas in the above chart as being small value areas or sideways price movements above and below a shifting control price.

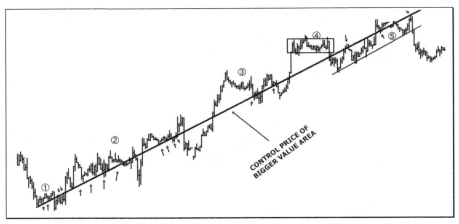

FIGURE 21: MOVING CONTROL PRICE

This is the same exact chart as the previous. Instead of marking the value areas on it, I have drawn the moving control price of what will be the bigger value area on this chart. Notice how the "1" to "5" value areas gravitate around this pivotal support and resistance line. The "1" small value area at the beginning of the upwards move has the control price running through its middle. It gravitates above and below it as shown by the small arrows. The "2" shifting value area's low provides strong additional meaning to this control price as shown by the arrows.

This value area stays above the control price. The "3" value area adds more validity to the control price by printing its excess price below it. The "4" and "5" value areas provide even further meaning to this diagonal line by populating price areas right below and right above it. Just as with value area "1", the control price runs through the middle of these two.

Notice that I have modified the value areas "4" and "5". If on the first chart, prior to marking the control price I saw appropriate to draw those small value areas as horizontal ones, after seeing the control price on the chart and the way price gravitates around it in that area, I changed my mind and made that value area "5" a shifting value.

There is no meaningful initiating strong move upwards, away from value area "4". As with everything I have presented so far, try not to over analyze things you see on your charts, use the logic described in the first chapter where I have presented the control price and what you should focus on when marking it. Do not seek mathematical precision.

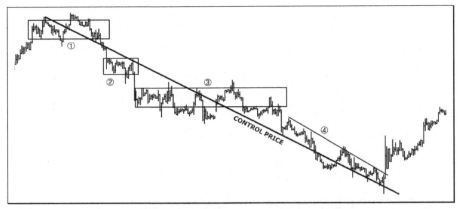

FIGURE 22: CONTROL PRICE IN DOWNTREND

Another example of control price that cuts through the value areas. The "4" value area is a shifting one. Its lower boundary coincides with the control price as you can see. The important thing to remember is that the control price you draw on your chart should have trading activity surrounding it from both sides. This trading activity develops value. As with the previous chart, if I did not have the control price plotted on it, maybe I would have chosen to break the number "4" shifting value area into two separate, smaller, horizontal value areas.

Seeing the chart with the control price on it and how the price action just flows slowly downwards, I thought this way of marking the value area gives more validity to the control price than by drawing two small horizontal values instead. Drawn this way, you can see that the shifting value area's low coincides with the control price.

This makes you feel more confident that you have identified a strong control price of the bigger value area. In both examples, the trend direction changes following these shifting value areas. This is no coincidence. We will discuss this in the next chapter.

On the same note, there will be occasions when price movements become too erratic because of fundamental news that comes out. At times, you will find it hard to distinguish a satisfactory moving control price because the market is all over the place making huge vertical moves up and down.

The normal behavior of price is to go in one direction, stop, consolidate, give value to price, correct in the other direction and then resume the initial direction. If you see vertical strong moves up and down the chart that make it very hard to find a logical moving control then you either go to a higher, more calm, timeframe or you find something else to trade.

VALUE HIGH, LOW AND EXCESS

Just as with the value areas presented in the first chapter, these big value areas have upper, lower limits and excess price too. The logic behind them is exactly the same, the only difference being that you are now trying to find the boundaries and the control of an area of price comprised of multiple, horizontal and shifting value areas to construct the bigger value of price.

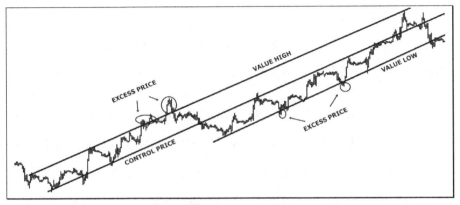

FIGURE 23: THE BIG VALUE

See how the value area high, the value area low and the excess price show themselves just as in horizontal value areas. The difference is that this area of price contained in the value is very big. The value areas that you see gravitating around the control price in this chart are actually very mature, standalone value areas of price themselves. Notice how the excess forms above value high and below value low, exactly as it happens in the conventional, horizontal value areas. Please notice where the blank space is located inside the value area. At the beginning of the big value, on the left of the chart, we see trading activity above the control price and a lot of blank space below it.

This is characteristic for an uptrend. This shows us that the buyers are in complete control, the demand is greater than the supply. Remember what I said at the beginning of this material, that the market is looking to facilitate trading between the buyer and the seller. If there is zero trading activity below the control price, this means that the market is not succeeding in facilitating trading at those price areas. It also means that the buyer is very strong there and the seller is not interested in stepping into the market at these price levels. As soon as the price touches the control, the buyer steps in to push the price up.

On the value side above the control price however, the situation is very different. The market does facilitate trading in these price areas as we can see a lot of trading activity going on. These price levels spark interest from the sellers who step into the market. Half way through the value area the situation changes. There is now a lot of trading activity below the control price and zero activity above it. This means that price has gone far enough north for the sellers to consider it as a trading opportunity.

Therefore they increase the supply, positioning their selling orders around the control price, instead of the value area high, as it happened in the first part of the big value. This being a clear uptrend with the buyers not succeeding to move the price past the control to visit the value area high anymore, is not a good sign for this uptrend. More about how to judge the end of a trend in the next chapter.

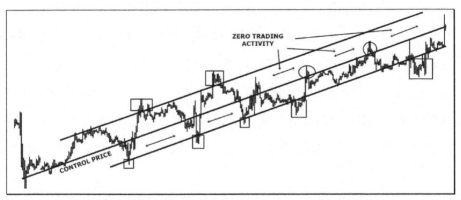

FIGURE 24: BIG VALUE AREA EXAMPLE

See the chart above. We have the control price which we draw first by looking for an area where price seems to be stopping, turning, making value above and below it. We then proceed to draw the high and low of the value area to include the bulk of trading just like described in the first chapter.

We then move on to mark the excess price above the value high and below the value low. Notice how at the start of the up move there is much smaller trading activity below the control than there is above. The market is not facilitating trading in this area as the seller is not interested. It is not viewed as an advantageous price area. This is showing us clearly that the buyers outnumber the sellers. The excess price location also gives clues regarding supply and demand dynamics.

There is great demand at value area low, where we see buying tails and excess every time the price reaches that area. The supply, or selling orders are observed at the value area high where the excess is. Remember that excess shows the footprint of the long term trader. Just by counting the number of excess levels above and below value and observing how much time price has spent above value, as compared to below value, gives clear indication on who is winning the battle at this moment. Again, the situation soon changes and through the last part of the big value area, the area with the least trading activity moves above the control price. The market is not facilitating trading in that area above the control, marked with those double arrows.

Why? Because there are no buyers there anymore. The trading activity remains confined between the control and value area low, providing us with clues about supply and demand location once again. The supply is now at the control price and the demand at value area low. Furthermore, we see rejection of the control price in two occasions with those swift spikes marked with circles on the chart.

The fact that all trading activity is happening below the control price in an uptrend, and that the sellers enter the market aggressively at the control price is clear indication that the uptrend is about to terminate.

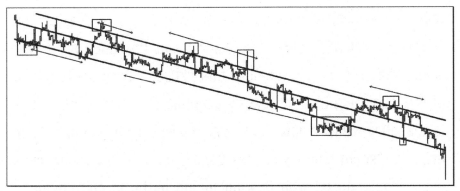

FIGURE 25: THE BIG VALUE IN DOWNTREND

This is a downtrend as the value areas are moving down. Notice that there are more excess price zones above value than below it. This is characteristic in a downtrend as the sellers are in charge and show this aggressively when price leaves the value area. It is too much of a good price for them to miss. As a result they enter the market increasing supply at those areas marked with a rectangle above value.

The control price is obviously the middle line. The double headed arrows you see on the chart parallel to the value area limits show each value area inside the big value. We will be discussing a lot more about these big value areas throughout the book. For now, all I want is for you to learn how to draw them on your charts.

> THEREFORE, PLEASE STOP READING AT THIS POINT AND TURN TO YOUR TRADING PLATFORM ONCE AGAIN. STUDY HOW VALUE MOVES THROUGHOUT THE CHART DIRECTIONALLY AND HOW IT GRAVITATES AROUND A CONTROL. DRAW THAT CONTROL PRICE AND DRAW THE BIG VALUE'S LIMITS AND EXCESS. MAKE OBSERVATIONS OF WHAT IS PRICE SHOWING IN AN UPTREND AS COMPARED TO A DOWNTREND IN TERMS OF EXCESS AND TRADING ACTIVITY LOCATION. COMPARE THE EXCESS ABOVE TO THE ONE BELOW VALUE, NOTICE THE ZONES WITH THE LEAST TRADING ACTIVITY INSIDE THE VALUE AREA, OBSERVE THE SHIFTING VALUES INSIDE THE BIG VALUE AND SEE IF YOU CAN MAKE A CONNECTION BETWEEN ALL OF THIS AND THE END OF THE TREND.

CHAPTER FOUR - USE IN TRADING

Presuming that you have done the practice and now have a pretty good idea on how to identify what has been presented above, we have finally arrived to the more fun part of the material where I will try to explain the best I can how to take advantage of all these concepts in actual trading. Before I get into that though, there is one more thing I need to cover. That is how to judge the rejection of a certain price level in the market.

REJECTION

Conventional ways of judging rejection of a price area by reading the price action requires the use of candlestick or bar patterns and price patterns. I am going to present the ones that are most effective in doing this and see if we can find a common denominator for them.

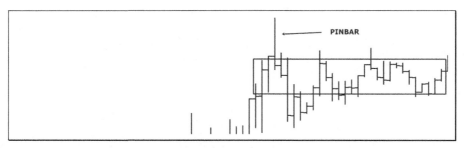

FIGURE 26: PIN BAR SHOWING REJECTION

This single bar that you see there protruding away from the surrounding price action is called a "pin bar" and is amongst the most effective ways to confirm a reversal at a certain point in the market. If you are using candlestick charts instead of bar charts you might know it better as a "hammer".

They are one and the same. It really does not matter how you call them. It shows rejection of the level above it because it opens low, inside the surrounding price action, it travels higher, finds the resistance level and comes back down quickly, closing lower than its open, well inside the surrounding price. If you are not completely new to trading you surely have seen it many times on your charts or even used it in trading.

What gives this pin bar power is the fact that it stands out from the surrounding price action. There is nothing to the left and nothing to the right of it. Notice that I have engulfed into a rectangle its surrounding price action. Are you starting to see where am I going with this? Yes, the surrounding price is the value area and the pin bar itself is the tail in the excess price of the value area that shows sellers entering the market to move price back to value.

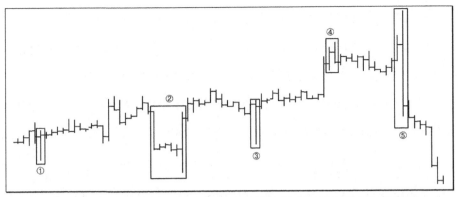

FIGURE 27: BARS AND BAR PATTERNS THAT INDICATE REJECTION

Those labeled on the above chart from "1" to "5" are all effective bars and bar patterns that will indicate rejection of a price level. The "1" and "3" are pin bars that we have just covered. The "2" is a bar pattern, or candlestick pattern if that is what you use on your charts, that has the following logic behind it. Price moves swiftly down with that first bar in the rectangle. Price finds a strong support there, printing small sideways bars to indicate that this level of price is not attractive for the sellers. The last bar goes below the tiny bars only to find strong demand and reverse to continue upwards with force.

This indicates that the demand is greater than supply at this price level and that the buyers have entered the market. What is the common denominator with the pin bar presented above?

The value of price is that small sideways area with the small bars. The price moves below value attracting strong demand that exhibits responsive trading, moving the price back to value at first and then taking it one step further, moving the price upwards, away from value with initiative activity.

We can easily call the dip below value of the last bar a tail in excess price. All these bar patterns are most effective at price extremes, where there is no recent trading activity surrounding them. The "4" bar pattern holds its power in the fact that the second bar goes up beyond the high of the first bar only to close back down, well within the lower half of the first candle. This is again just another way of looking at a value area with excess price above it. The "5" is an engulfing bar pattern.

The second bar completely engulfs the first one which shows increasing volatility, and that in turn, shows sellers have entered the market. Only an increase of supply at that price level could have made that price bar so big. Again, if we draw a rectangle there, identifying the clearly visible value, we can easily consider this pattern as a value with a tail above and an initiating move below value.

FIGURE 28: REVERSAL PRICE PATTERNS

The first on the left is a multiple top price congestion pattern where price touches the upper boundary of the sideways movement two or more times prior to a strong down move. You might now this as a double top or triple top price pattern, the difference being how many times the price tests the value high area before it gives up and goes strongly in the other direction. If the distinct tops or spikes to the same level of price marked with those circles would have moved a little more outside of the surrounding price they would have been in excess price territory above value area. They are usually found there, outside above value area. We do however have a selling tail there. The value is the rectangle. The second one is a head and shoulders pattern.

The first and last circles are the shoulders of the pattern with the higher circle in the middle being the head of the pattern. This is perhaps the most popular of the reversal price patterns. The idea is in this particular case to sell when price goes below the neckline of the pattern, which coincides with the value area low on this chart. As you can easily see, this too is nothing more than a value area with excess price above it.

Why use the value area rejection method? I did mention earlier in this material why it is important to focus more on the underlying concepts behind the price movements than on the lines you draw on your chart.

Memorizing a price or bar pattern like the ones above is a simple thing to do and surely more tempting or at hand than thorough analysis of the supply and demand through price movements. But what do you do if, when you are preparing to enter the market, you do not see any of these conventional rejection patterns? This happens often. The interaction of the price with the level you are waiting to be rejected will not result in a conventional price or candlestick pattern every time. Looking at the last example above, maybe price will make three left shoulders before it develops the head in the head and shoulders pattern. Maybe, the double or triple top will not be as textbook as you might expect and you find yourself having trouble identifying it because the market is very volatile, very noisy.

Does this mean that there is no rejection? No, it means that there is no easy recognizable pattern or that there is no conventional pattern at all. As long as you can identify a value area with excess price or tails on the side with the level you are waiting to see rejection of, you are good to go. You do not have to wait for a pattern that might not happen. Also, the fact that a value area takes more time to form than a single bar or candle gives this approach much more validity than any other.

We are going to use this rejection approach in the following way. At the price level we want to trade, we go to a lower timeframe than the one we intend to trade on and we wait for a small value area with excess and/or tail to form. The excess or tail will show rejection of the price level. It would be preferable to have a tail because it shows rejection more clearly, more swiftly. Then, on the same lower timeframe we wait for an initiative move away from the value area and, at the same time, away from the level that price has rejected. We do not enter a trade when the initiative move breaks the value limit because there are many false breakouts during the value developing process that can be difficult to spot in real trading.

Maybe what looks to be initiative move away from value area quickly returns back into value and tests again our rejected level. We trade if the initiative move is confirmed by a responsive move back to value followed by a subsequent initiative move in the same direction as the first. I will illustrate this shortly.

FRAMEWORK

Even if you, after reading this material, decide for some reason that it doesn't suit your trading style or you are still convinced that you can make better trading judgments using other tools than these presented here, you will always need to trade by taking into account the big picture. It is just silly to go to the five minutes charts for example and trade blindly off of them, without knowing what is happening on the higher timeframes.

The higher timeframes have a big influence on the price movements from the lower timeframes. Whatever your trading system is, you absolutely must go to the next higher timeframe and draw the support and resistance levels on it. It is guaranteed that this will keep you out of many losing trades.

The value area concept will provide extremely powerful support and resistance. You can trade their rejection on the lower timeframes or just as guidelines for better trading decisions. They will provide the bigger picture of price, the market structure, so that trading decisions will always be the best and most informed that you can make.

FIGURE 29: VALUE AREA ON A HIGHER TIMEFRAME

See this chart above. On the daily timeframe we have this absolutely huge horizontal value area. Assuming that you are more of a swing trader and you like to trade from the four hour charts, marking the value area on the daily chart would have served you extremely well when price got back up in value in that area pointed by the arrows on the lower right of the chart.

Looking at the four hour timeframe price movements alone, would have led you to believe that there will be a bigger pullback to the downside after the strong, aggressive bullish move. That is because this big horizontal value area is not visible on this timeframe. It is simply too big to see it all. The bigger pullback did not happen however because price crawled back inside value and the value area low acted as a very strong support for price, as you can see. Not to mention that you could have predicted the aggressive bullish move towards value in the following way. Value attracts price. When price moves away from value a trading opportunity is created. As I said before, price moving away from value is initiative behavior. I have described how an initiative move away from value should look like. Do you see any strong initiative move there on the break of value to the downside? No, there isn't one. There is a slow shifting of value to the downside which progresses only until huge demand is met at that big low to the left of the chart marked with a small rectangle. To sum this up :

1. We have a break of value to the downside which is not convincing at all. The break move does not bear the characteristics of an initiative move away from value. It is a slow shifting value area. Remember me saying that usually the price direction changes after these type of value areas

2. We know that value attracts price so we can imagine that such a weak move away from value will have responsive buying activity to get the price back in value

3. We see those low swings on the left of the chart. They are buying tails. As said before, these tails act as very strong support and resistance levels because they are the footprint of the long term trader entering the market. They show supply and demand levels.

To demonstrate the clear footprint of the long term trader entering the market at this level please look at the aggressive bullish move that pushes the price quickly inside value. If you remember, I said clearly that a move away with force from value area is the long term trader taking initiative. A move back to the value area is a responsive behavior that is not as forceful as the initiative. You can see that the buyers step into the market, and in only one day, they push the price back to value.

Does this look as responsive move back to value? It certainly doesn't. It is powerful, initiative strong move from the longer term buyer who saw the opportunity to buy at a low price according to his analysis. As far as he is concerned, he did not enter the market in response to initiative move away from value, he took the initiative and moved the price away from a bigger value area's high on his timeframe. You see that initiative and responsive behavior highly depends on the perspective each has.

This is one example where, doing a simple analysis on a higher timeframe than the one you are trading on, would have been a great help. It would have provided you with the much needed framework. In this exact situation, even if it would not have convinced you to buy this pair at the excess tail level, it would have certainly convinced you not to sell there and that is a big plus.

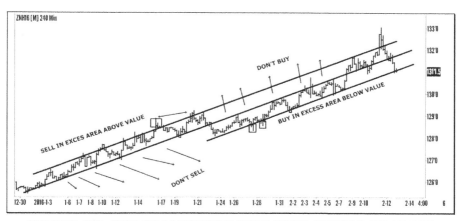

FIGURE 30: THE FRAMEWORK PROVIDES BETTER TRADING DECISIONS

This is another example of how doing your analysis of the bigger picture can determine you to make the best trading decisions possible. If day trading on the lower timeframes is what suits you best then you must start by doing analysis of price action on a more relevant timeframe such as the four hours one. After you have found the bigger value on the higher timeframe you can trade with more certainty on the 15 or 30 minutes for example. This provides the best framework possible for you to trade in. You will have a clear picture of where is best to sell, where is best to buy. As a rule, seek to buy in excess below value or in the bottom value area, between the value area low and the control.

Seek to sell in excess territory above value or in the top value area, between the value high and the control. Definitely do not buy when price is in excess territory above value and do not sell when it is in excess below value. As I said at the beginning of this book, we need to behave like the long term traders do.

We buy and sell where the odds are in our favor, where there is the greatest probability that price will do what we expect it to do. That is why we must sell where the greatest supply is, at the top of the value area or in in excess above it. Conversely, we must buy where the greatest demand is, in excess below value area or at the bottom of it.

Please notice on this chart the tail above value marked with a rectangle. That on its own is a strong supply zone, or a strong resistance for price, however you want to call it. From there price travels back to the mean and then back up to the value area high. The value area high being a diagonal line that travels up the chart, the price level where it gets touched is roughly the same as that of the tail just below. This is confluence. If you have read some of my material before or you have been trading the markets you realize the meaning of confluence and how powerful it can be. The value area high and the tail at the same price level is a confluence of factors. It gives this price level additional strength and it gives you two reasons to sell the rejection of it.

The first one is that price has touched the value area high and there is a good possibility it will reverse to the control at least. The second one is that the price level also coincides with the tail that happened earlier which gives it additional resistance. The sellers will have one extra reason to position their selling orders there, right at the value area high, increasing supply and increasing your chances to have a winning short trade.

If you wouldn't have done this analysis on the bigger timeframe, you wouldn't have known that there is confluence at this price level. Perhaps you wouldn't have had sufficient confidence to enter a sell order there.

TREND IDENTIFICATION AND CHANGE

"The trend is your friend". You have probably heard this saying a million times. I know I have. Well, if it is our friend, the most logical thing to do would be to get to know it. The conventional way of identifying a trend using price action is to mark the highs and lows that price makes on the chart. When it prints higher highs and higher lows we are in an uptrend. When it prints lower highs and lower lows we have a downtrend in front of us. When it goes from higher highs and higher lows to lower highs and lower lows we have an uptrend turning into a downtrend. I have covered this type of price action analysis in some of my earlier books. For those of you who are not familiar with it, I will illustrate it.

FIGURE 31: TREND IDENTIFICATION WITH HIGHS AND LOWS

This is a clear downtrend. The down arrows point to the lower highs of the trend while the up arrows point to the lower lows. The downtrend turns into an uptrend when price makes and confirms a higher low at the lower right side of the chart. That higher low is only confirmed by the following move upwards.

This way of judging a trend is powerful. However, doing the value area, excess, control price and initiative or responsive moves analysis offers a lot more information regarding the trend. Don't think of it as a substitute for the method above. Use them both to confirm the same thing. They can be complementary.

If you come to the same conclusion by doing two different types of analysis you will have much more confidence when taking a trade. Let's see what the same chart looks like when marking all you have been learning so far.

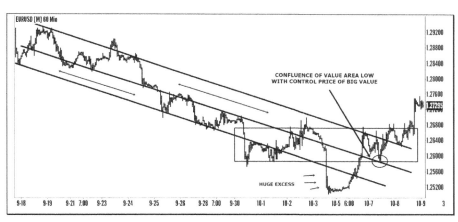

FIGURE 32: TREND ANALYSIS WITH VALUE

I have drawn the big value area along with its limits and control price. What observations can be made by analyzing each component?

THE VALUE AREAS. Each value area is taking shape at a price level lower than the previous. Clear indication of a downtrend

THE CONTROL PRICE. It has a downwards slope. Another indication of a downtrend

THE LOCATION OF TRADING ACTIVITY. At the end of the chart, on the lower right, we can see that the trading activity moves in the top part of the value area, between the control and the value high. This is uncharacteristic for a downtrend.

Additionally, the price rotations are becoming narrower, it is starting to rotate between the control and value high. In a downtrend, when price rotations become small and they happen in the upper part of the value area, the trend is most likely to end.

The narrower the rotations, the bigger the break of value will be. Why is this? Because the market is becoming too efficient in facilitating trading between buyers and sellers. It doesn't have to travel from value area low to value area high and back to find the demand and the supply. These two are now found in a very tight price area between the value high and the control price. There is only one outcome possible when this happens. Someone wins the war, the rotations stop and price moves away from the area.

There is no trading activity below the control price so the market has to move higher and find another control to gravitate in order to facilitate trading on both sides of the value area. Most likely what is now the top of the value area between the control and the value high, will become the bottom of a new value area with an upwards direction. All this is a strong clue that the trend is about to change

The excess price. We can see huge excess below the lower boundary of the value. The further price moves down, away from value area low, in excess territory, the bigger the possibility that the current value or trend will be broken.

Why? Because it brings in more demand. The lower that price goes in excess territory the greater attraction from buyers it has. If it goes far enough, like it happened in this situation, price will be considered more and more attractive and the demand will increase significantly. The big excess price is another clear indication that the value or trend is about to be broken. And we can realize this sooner than we would have with the conventional method

CONFLUENCE. I have engulfed in the rectangle the last value of the downtrend and extended it to the right to capture the price activity in the top value area, just before it breaks the value to the upside. You can see how price, after that long excess below value, climbs back up, in the top part of the value area, but also inside the territory of the last value of the trend, or the last value of the bigger value if you like. We have a confluence there of price finding support at the control price and at the last value area's low at the same time. This is the level circled out on the chart.

We have all the reasons in the world to trade this as soon as a lower timeframe shows a rejection of this confluence zone. All the analysis we have done indicates that the downtrend is about to terminate and we have a confluence zone of two powerful support areas.

Another trading approach in this situation would have been to find a support zone when price was in that huge excess below value and buy its rejection. Why? Any move away from value creates a trading opportunity. Our goal is to speculate market imbalance between supply and demand. Buying that low, well outside of value, would be a great trading opportunity with very low risk and a high chance of success.

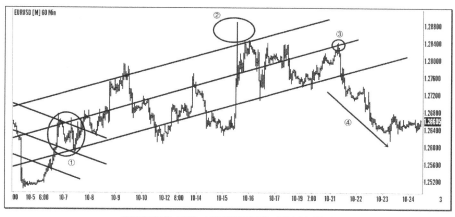

FIGURE 33: UPTREND CHANGE

This is a continuation of price action from the previous chart. See the area circled on the left side of the chart and marked with a "1". Those are the narrow rotations between the control and the value high of the previous big value area or the downtrend. They have now become part of the next big value that price has developed. They are situated in the bottom part of this value area. Notice the big tail the sellers have made at the "2" circle. Clear indication that supply has been met at this price level.

I want you to go through the following thinking process when looking at this chart. Value is moving up, the control price is pointing up so we are in an uptrend for the moment. The trading activity is taking place on both sides of the control, we cannot see a clear difference in the volume of activity on the two sides of the value area. This indicates that the uptrend is not very strong. It is probably just a short move upwards, a correction of price in a bigger downtrend on a higher timeframe.

Why do I say this? Because, as already discussed, a healthy, powerful uptrend will always have a clearly visible difference between the amount of trading activity on the top and bottom parts of the value. The trading activity would be greater on the top part in an uptrend because the buyers are in control of the market, pushing the price rather quickly upwards whenever it travels at or near the value low.

The thinking goes on. Up to this point, the analysis you have done so far is telling you that there is a clear uptrend but not a very strong one. You see the big tail at point "2" that the sellers are making and you immediately think to yourself that this is yet another odd price behavior in an uptrend. The buyers should be making these type of strong tails below value in an uptrend, not the sellers. The price hasn't gone that much above value in excess price to bring in very strong supply and justify this type of sharp tail. At point "3" you see price finding resistance at the control price after it has traded in the bottom part of the value. There are sellers there as you see price going fast towards the value low. At this time you should be preparing for a break of the value to the downside. You have identified clear signs to make this judgment call.

Soon, the sellers take the initiative and move the price away from value at "4". At this point, to find the new control that price will most likely gravitate around, you need to wait for a new small value area to take shape after the initiative selling that took place at the "4" price area. It will be situated below the last small horizontal value area in the uptrend. I am talking about the value between "2" and "3".

After this new value has formed following the initiating move below value and trend change, try to draw the new control with a downwards slope finding a pivotal support and resistance that connects the value low of the last small value in the trend with the new found value. As time passes you would have to adjust it a little bit but this initial drawing will provide you with clear insight regarding future price movements.

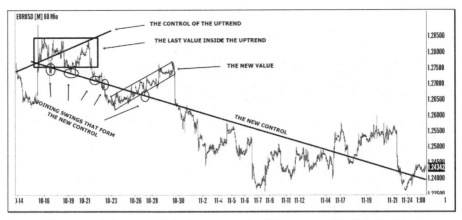

FIGURE 34: FINDING THE NEW CONTROL PRICE EARLY

This is the continuation of the previous chart. After the initiative selling away from the big uptrend value price makes a small shifting value. At this point you need to start looking for the new control of price. Try to find it by joining the low of the last value area in the uptrend with some price rotations inside the new value. Don't worry if this is not completely clear at this point or it is hard to find. You will adjust it latter when the price movements will give more clues.

The important thing is that this will provide early insight of the area that future price movements will gravitate.

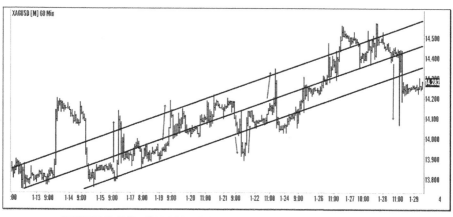

FIGURE 35: CHANGE IN INITIATIVE MOVEMENTS

See this uptrend. Notice who has the initiative inside the value area. The normal behavior in such an uptrend is for the buyers to make initiative strong moves away from small value inside the big value area. When the sellers start to make more initiative swift moves in an uptrend than the buyers you can safely assume that the trend is about to end.

Observe how, throughout the value, the buyers are making swift, forceful strong moves upwards that make the price move away fast from the chunks of value. Excluding the last move at the end of the chart, the only time that the sellers manage to take initiative and move price away from value is in the area with the down arrow beside it, where it moves price in excess below value. That is short lived as buyers quickly step in and push the price back to value. Towards the top right of the chart, the price has gone high enough to find strong supply of selling orders. This is clearly shown by the huge initiative move down away from value marked with the long down arrow next to it.

Think of initiative moves away from value as vertical or almost vertical quick moves of price. Paying attention at who is taking initiative in moving the price away from the small areas of value inside the bigger value provides additional help in judging the change in direction of price.

One more thing to add to your arsenal is to open up your charts and observe what kind of price movements happened in the past almost every time the market has changed its direction, changing the trend in the process. Please notice "Figure 19" once more. See the shifting value areas "1" and "4" and how price changes direction following them. They are both composed of three waves of price so to speak, with each wave going only a little further upwards than the previous one.

This develops three distinct spikes that you can clearly see by looking at the upper boundary of each value and seeing that it was touched on three occasions. Further, I need you to look at the last horizontal value at the lower right of the "Figure 5" once more and observe what happened after it. Yes, the trend changed its direction. That value area is special because of its huge excess. See how the price climbs back inside value after the huge move in excess and respects the value boundaries. You will see this as a shifting type of value also at the end of a trend. The value shifts slowly in one direction, the price prints huge excess and brings the other trader in the market to change direction.

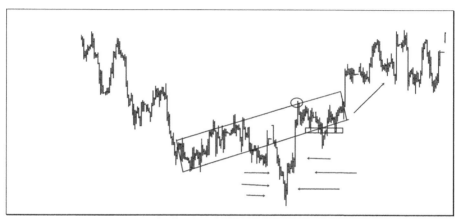

FIGURE 36: SHIFTING VALUE WITH HUGE EXCESS ENDING TREND

This is the type of value I am talking about. It has the same meaning as the horizontal one in "Figure 5". If you are familiar with reversal price patterns like the "head and shoulders" pattern discussed earlier would you consider this a "head and shoulders" reversal pattern when you see it on your chart? Probably not. It might not look as a textbook, easy recognizable pattern but it shows us the same underlying dynamic between supply and demand a "head and shoulders" would do. This is exactly the reason I say not to get hung up on patterns and mechanical trading.

Think of this as a shifting value of price with big excess. I need you to look now once again at "Figure 28" and notice the first value in the rectangle on the left side of the chart. Notice the vertical strong move preceding it and the rotations inside the value itself. Observe that they are very close to one another, there is not much space at all between them. The price is making many rotations between the high and low of value within a short period of time. It can make only two rotations, three or more. The important thing to consider is the strong, preceding vertical move and the time spent between rotations to be small when compared with the most recent value areas inside the big trend or big value.

These three types of value will give you important insight regarding a change in direction of price. When you see them in an uptrend or a downtrend, take note of them and put them in context. The expectation is that they will be the end of the current trend or big value the price is trading in. Use them along with all the other tools presented above to make the best judgments possible.

> IT'S TIME FOR ME TO ASK YOU AGAIN TO GO TO YOUR CHARTS AND PRACTICE WHAT YOU HAVE READ. MAKE OBSERVATIONS OF YOUR OWN. DO THE ANALYSIS OF THE BIG VALUE AREAS ON YOUR CHARTS. SEE HOW STUDYING THE VALUE INSIDE THE BIG VALUE, THE TRADING ACTIVITY LOCATION, THE EXCESS, THE CONTROL, THE INITIATIVE MOVEMENTS, THE THREE TYPES OF VALUE THAT HAVE JUST BEEN DISCUSSED PROVIDES YOU WITH THE MUCH NEEDED INSIGHT REGARDING THE PRICE ACTION MOVEMENTS ON YOUR CHARTS AND THE TRENDS THEY CREATE, THE BIG VALUE THEY CREATE, HOW THEY MOVE FROM ONE CONTROL TO ANOTHER.

SUPPORT, RESISTANCE, REJECTION

So far we have used the price action concepts presented in this material to see the market structure or framework on the higher timeframe, and for trend identification and trend change. This, as you will see for yourself, will greatly improve your decisions making process and your overall trading results. I hope you have done the practice by now and that you are getting familiar with what has been presented so far. If not, don't rush to the end of the book, take your time and read the book again from the beginning until all is clearly understood. All the price action concepts are explained in detail, you just need to be aware that this is a learning process.

If you are completely new to this kind of trading with the naked chart, it will naturally take some time until you get good at it. Do the work, practice, practice some more and you will see how your trading improves.

Now, I want to discuss a little bit about the powerful support and resistance levels that a value area will provide and how to take advantage of this knowledge in real trading.

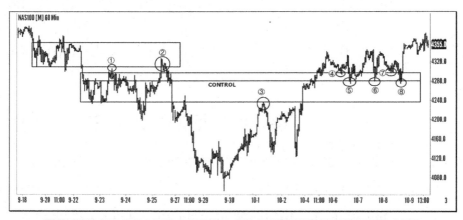

FIGURE 37: VALUE ACTING AS STRONG SUPPORT AND RESISTANCE

See how value creates support and resistance zones for price. This has to do with what has been discussed throughout the book about supply and demand and how the sellers position themselves at the value high and buyers at value low.

Once these levels get broken, there is a change is supply and demand dynamics. Think of this as a war between the buyers and the sellers. Those who manage to push the market through a level of price where the other was exhibiting interest, conquer that level and set their entry orders there for when price comes back to revisit the level.

This constant friction between buyers and sellers turn the value area high, low and control price into very powerful support turning into resistance after it has been broken, and very powerful resistance for price that turns into support once broken. Notice the two value areas on the chart above. I have extended their territory to intersect with future price movements.

At first we see the low of the first value area on the left proving resistance for price at the "1" and "2" turning points. At "3" we see the price encountering sellers or strong supply at the low of the second value on the chart. Once the low of this value has been broken to the downside, it turned into resistance. At "4" and "7" we see price finding support at value high and at "5", "6" and "8", we see it finding strong support at the control price of the value area. You will see this kind of behavior on any chart and any timeframe, again and again. This is just how price moves, from one value to another, from one support and resistance zone to another.

If you are not a complete beginner to trading, you have

probably plotted support and resistance lines on your charts before. This is how they are constructed. If you go anywhere on your charts right now and draw a pivotal support and resistance line as described when the control price was presented, you will find multiple value high below it, value low above it and the occasional excess price and tails from time to time piercing it.

We are going to use the value area high, the value area low and control price to enter a trade, exit a trade and place protective stops above or below them. More on this in the final chapter where we put it all together to formulate a complete trading plan with clear setups to look for.

Besides the fact that value attracts price and provides strong support and resistance it has another, extremely beneficial characteristic. When price goes back to value and shows acceptance, it will, 8 out of 10 times, fill the value area.

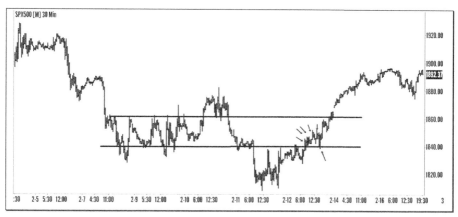

FIGURE 38: VALUE AREA FILLING

See this chart above. Price breaks away from value to the downside. Observe what is happening when it returns to value. The value low provide strong resistance on three occasions pushing the price back down. There are sellers there. The buyers however do not give up easily and, on the forth move they manage to push the price back inside value, above the value low. At this point, in order to take advantage of this powerful concept of value area filling, we need to see clear rejection from price of the value low which is now acting as strong support. Only then we would enter a buying order with the target being the value high.

To see this rejection, we need to go to a lower timeframe. Remember what was discussed about rejection earlier. We need a value area with a tail piercing the value low to develop.

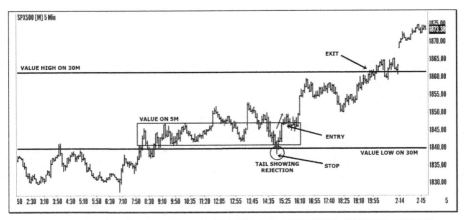

FIGURE 39: TRADE ENTRY WITH REJECTION OF SUPPORT

And we have it. Price develops a value area on the five minutes chart as expected. It is showing clear rejection of the support value low exhibited by the tail in excess, piercing the value low and quickly retracing back to the five minutes chart value area. The tail is the one marked with a circle on the above chart. The rejection requirement has been met. All you need to do know in order to take advantage of the value area filling concept is to wait for the five minutes value high to be broken above and for price to retrace back to it before filing the bigger value on the thirty minutes chart.

That is what happens as price breaks the resistance of value high on the five minutes marked with the small up arrow, only to retrace at this level before continuing upwards to the 30m value area high. The value high of the smaller timeframe value is now acting as support for price. This is your entry point. The protective stop for your order will be set below the tail and the take profit level will be at the touch of the value high of the 30m chart.

Why set the protective stop below the tail? No matter what type of trading you are using, you need to set the stop where price has the least probability of touching it. There is strong demand at the tail, this will keep price away from that level. Just above the tail, there is the value low of the 30 minutes chart which is another strong support at this moment for price. The market will have a very tough time trying to touch our protective stop level because the buyer are present in that area and they will increase demand each time the market visits the surroundings.

On top of this, the supply would not be strong enough to win the war with demand in this price area. Price has to travel further up to the value high of the 30m chart to find increased supply. That is the area where the selling orders would be. Putting one or more support or resistance levels between your entry and your stop is definitely the way to go. So waiting for a value area with a tail to judge a rejection of a bigger value low or bigger value high will also provide the possibility to set a protective stop where price cannot go.

This will increase the chances of your trades going in the desired direction, towards your take profit level. The take profit will be set at the other value boundary, in this particular case, at the value high of the 30m chart. Price might go and will, often times, go further than that rather than retrace, but it will rarely go through the value boundary easily. It will stop there for a while, trade below and above this value limit keeping you in the trade for a long time. Possibly even more than a week if you are trading on a higher timeframe. Remember that you are in this trade because of a concept called value area filling. When the price has reached your take profit set at the other value limit, the value has been filled. You are better off exiting and waiting patiently for a new setup.

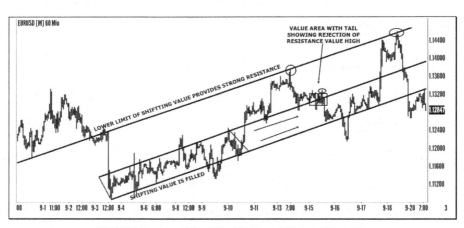

FIGURE 40: SHIFTING VALUE IS FILLED

The same type of trading can be applied to shifting value areas also. First of observe on the above chart how the low of the value area on the left of the chart of the chart acts as a resistance for future price action. Notice those small circles where price touched the value low and retraces.

Secondly, the price action engulfed in a rectangle is a shifting value area. Looking at its extension, we can see that price broke above it, found strong resistance and reversed only to find support at the high of the value in the rectangle. After a few tries, price manages to creep back inside value and to show rejection of the value area high, which has now turned into resistance. We then follow the same procedure as in the example above on a lower timeframe.

Notice in both trade examples that the rejection value is rather small in size, giving us the possibility to enter a trade with a smaller risk than the potential reward. This is critical.

Do not enter trades where the distance from the entry to the protective stop is greater than the distance from the entry to the take profit level. They risk you take on for every trade must always be smaller than the potential reward.

This is how you become profitable consistently. With a risk always smaller than the reward, you will not have to worry about those two times out of ten where the market doesn't fill the value area as it should.

Sometimes, when the big value area that you are expecting to get filled, is not very complex, meaning that is very narrow or small in size or it doesn't have many price rotations in it, rejection might not have time to become clear on a lower timeframe.

You might see that price is almost trading vertically and no clear small value area with a tail can be seen. Move on. There is no trade there. Look for developed value like the ones in the above examples. They are fairly wide, tall and composed of multiple price rotations. You can take advantage of this value filling concept even if you already have some trading plan that is working for you.

Incorporate this type of trading in it. Build around it using some of your own ideas.

> **YOU CAN START RIGHT NOW BY DOING SOME PRACTICE ON YOUR CHARTS, LOOKING AT THE VALUE AREAS, GOING TO A LOWER TIMEFRAME TO SEE THE REJECTION AND THEN THE FILLING OF THE VALUE AREA.**

CHAPTER FIVE - PUTTING IT TOGETHER

TIMEFRAMES

The first thing you need to do in order to prepare yourself for trading is to take a picture of the price movements on a higher timeframe than the one you intend on trading in. For example, if I want to trade on the one hour or the four hour charts I go to the daily timeframe and carefully draw the control and the value area on that chart. If I want to day trade on the 30 minutes and 15 minutes, I go to the four hours timeframe, identify the big value there and draw it on the chart. If I want to trade on the 5 minutes timeframe, I go to the one hour and make the value area analysis there. These timeframe correlations are not set in stone however.

When deciding on what higher timeframe you should use to draw the value on, look first at current price location on the timeframe you will be trading in. Then scroll back the same chart and try to put it into context. Is the current price movement part of an uptrend, a downtrend or is it part of a sideways movement? Remember the discussion about how the trend changes when the price starts to make value below in an uptrend and value above in a downtrend. Go to the next higher timeframe and find the location where price developed value that changed the trend. If you don't see it there, go to the next higher timeframe.

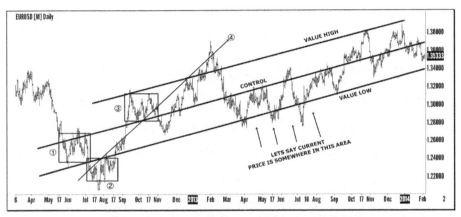

FIGURE 41: DRAWING THE BIG PICTURE

Let us assume, for example purposes, that you want to trade on the four hours chart and that current price is in the area pointed out by the arrows in the above chart. You go to the daily and try to find the context of the current price action. You see a downtrend there at the left of the chart that has been broken. The value area high of that trend has been broken by the initiative buyers following the number "2" value area on the chart. That is a strong initiative move that confirms the break and the end of the downtrend by printing value above. That is value area "3". Notice the "2" shifting value with big excess and remember what has been discussed earlier in the "trend change" section about the type of value areas that will most likely end the trend. See "Figure 36".

When we see that the value high of the downtrend has been broken, price has printed value above and that number "2" value area that strengthens our belief that the downtrend has ended, it automatically means that this is the area where the new control price is starting, the one that has relevance for the current price movements. How do we draw it? Of course, if we look at the four up arrows and see where we currently are, it is easy to draw the control because we already see past price gravitating above and below it.

As explained in the same "trend change" section earlier in the book, "figure 34", we can estimate where the control for the new trend will be, with very good probability of success, very early in the trend. We join the top of the last value in the downtrend that was surpassed by the new value, with the bottom of the higher value that changed the trend. The upwards diagonal line that results from this is, as you can see, is the control price for that big uptrend on the daily timeframe that lasted for two years. We have managed to find the control of the new uptrend, at the beginning of the trend, right after price made the value "3" and broke away from it. See the line labeled as "4" on the chart. That is a control price that resulted from joining the last value of the downtrend with the new value that broke the trend. I know that when we have discussed about how the trend changes earlier in the book, I said that you should join the last value of the trend with the new value above or below that broke the trend.

See what happens on this chart if we do that. There is some control there, but only to an extent. The control is very abrupt, almost vertical, it is unrealistic to think that price will spend a long time gravitating around a vertical line. What I meant was that you should join the last value of the trend that was surpassed by the new value, with the new value. In this chart, the initiative buying was so strong that price has surpassed the last two value areas of the downtrend.

In such situations we, of course, seek to estimate a more realistic control price that will last until the trend ends. We join the last value of the downtrend that got surpassed and is now acting as support, with the new value. As time goes by, if you observe that price is making rotations that stop and turn in an area just around the control and not exactly at it, you will need to adjust it to fit the price action. These will be minor adjustments though, so there is nothing to worry about.

Usually, the early control that you identify when the trend changes remains roughly the same throughout the whole trend.

As already said earlier in the material, you need to look for normal price behavior. You need to see price is making up and down rotations around a control. This is what constitutes a healthy trend, where both buyer and sellers are engaged.

When you see abnormal price behavior, where price is going almost vertically up or down for a sustained period of time, without rotations, do not try to figure out where the value is and where the control is. That sustained vertical move is caused by fundamental news. The market is not facilitating trading well.

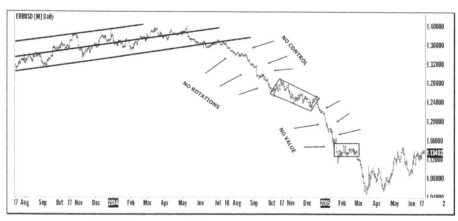

FIGURE 42: ABNORMAL PRICE BEHAVIOR

See what happened on the same daily chart after the uptrend value was broken to the downside. For almost a year, the sellers pushed price with force, almost vertically due to fundamental news that the euro is about to crash. The result of this? The market has not facilitated trading between buyers and sellers. The buyers were nowhere to be seen. Price did not make price rotations, did not make value area except for the two marked with a rectangle. There is no discernible value and no clear control with price gravitating up and down around it. No clear excess price or tails either.

Move away from this timeframe. Go to a lower one where all these things are present if you want to trade this currency pair. Do the value area analysis on a lower timeframe this and use an even lower one to trade on. Technical analysis works when people behave in predictable patterns, not on erratic moves in financial crisis.

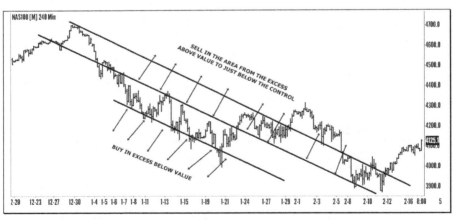

FIGURE 43: WHERE TO BUY AND WHERE TO SELL

The value area analysis on the higher timeframe will serve as framework for your trades on the lower timeframe. It will tell you where it is best to buy and where to sell in order to take only the highest probability trading setups.

Remember about the long term trader that moves the price with his big trading volumes and how he only enters the market at what he considers an advantageous price. What exactly is an advantageous price? It is a price area where the number of things that can go wrong and cause you a losing trade are minimal. The advantageous price gives you trading setups with the highest probability of success. The ideal advantageous price for a sell order would be the top of the market where price turns and starts to go down, never coming back to this top again. The ideal one for a buy order would be a bottom of the market where price starts to go up and never revisit the bottom until take profit level is hit. Unfortunately trading is not an ideal environment for you to accomplish this without taking on huge risks.

We can however, come close to this type of approach with the help of our value analysis. In a downtrend, like in the diagram above, we will consider as advantageous to sell in the area from the excess above value to just below the control price. An advantageous price to buy in a downtrend is the excess territory below value.

Why sell only in that area? Because we want to minimize risk and take only trades that have the highest probability of success. That is why we need to sell closer to the value high as possible. The further we drift away downwards from the value high when selling in a downtrend, the greater risk we take. Just because there is a strong downtrend it doesn't mean that price will go down all the time. Price will be making up and down rotations between the value high and value low. Why buy only in excess below value in a downtrend? Buying inside value in a downtrend would be too risky. Buying in excess below value in a downtrend will have minimal risk as price just doesn't have anywhere to go but up.

Remember that value attracts price. I am now going to lay out some guidelines for you to follow when preparing to trade on the lower timeframe.

I am now going to lay out some guidelines for you to follow when preparing to trade on the lower timeframe.

GUIDELINES

1. WHEN IN UPTREND, BUY IN THE AREA FROM THE EXCESS BELOW VALUE TO JUST ABOVE THE CONTROL. SELL IN THE EXCESS AREA ABOVE VALUE

2. WHEN IN DOWNTREND, SELL IN THE AREA FROM THE

EXCESS ABOVE VALUE TO JUST BELOW THE CONTROL. BUY IN THE EXCESS AREA BELOW VALUE

3. WHEN IN A SIDEWAYS MARKET, IN HORIZONTAL BIG VALUE, BUY IN THE AREA FROM THE EXCESS BELOW VALUE TO JUST ABOVE THE CONTROL PRICE. SELL IN THE AREA FROM THE EXCESS ABOVE VALUE TO JUST BELOW THE CONTROL PRICE OF THE VALUE

4. EVERY SINGLE TIME YOU FIND A POTENTIAL SETUP ON THE TIMEFRAME YOU ARE TRADING ON, BEFORE ENTERING THE TRADE, GO TO THE TIMEFRAME WHERE THE VALUE AREA ANALYSIS WAS DONE

5. LOOK AT THE CONTROL. SEE IF PRICE IS STILL GRAVITATING AROUND IT. IF NOT, MAKE THE MINOR ADJUSTMENTS NEEDED. MOVE IT ONE INCH HIGHER OR LOWER TO FIT THE PRICE ROTATIONS TURNING POINTS ABOVE AND BELOW IT

6. JUDGE THE HEALTH OF THE OVERALL VALUE. IS PRICE STILL MAKING TAILS BELOW VALUE IF IT IS AN UPTREND? IS IT STILL MAKING TAILS ABOVE VALUE IF IT IS A DOWNTREND? LOOK AT RECENT PRICE ACTION AND OBSERVE THIS

7. IF A DOWNTREND, IS THERE MORE TRADING ACTIVITY

BELOW THE CONTROL AS IT SHOULD BE? IF AN UPTREND, IS THERE MORE TRADING ACTIVITY ABOVE THE CONTROL, IN THE TOP PART OF VALUE AS THERE SHOULD BE? LOOK AT RECENT PRICE ACTION LEADING TO THE CURRENT PRICE AND MAKE A JUDGMENT

8. IF AN UPTREND, ARE THE BUYERS MAKING INITIATIVE STRONG MOVES AWAY FROM SMALL VALUE WITH THE SELLERS MAKING SLOW RESPONSIVE MOVES BACK TO VALUE AS THEY SHOULD? IF A DOWNTREND, ARE THE SELLERS MAKING STRONG INITIATIVE MOVES DOWNWARDS, AWAY FROM SMALL VALUE IN THE BIGGER VALUE, WHILE THE BUYERS ARE EXHIBITING SLOW RESPONSIVE ACTIVITY MOVING THE PRICE BACK UP TO SMALL VALUE? AS WITH THE ABOVE, SEEK THE CLUES IN THE RECENT PRICE ACTION LEADING UP TO WHERE THE CURRENT PRICE IS TRADING AT

9. IF TWO OR MORE OF THE LAST THREE POINTS ABOVE ARE NOT VALID, BE CAREFUL WITH YOUR TRADE. LOOK FOR SOLID REJECTION BEFORE ENTERING. SEEK TO PUT TWO SUPPORT OR RESISTANCE ZONES BETWEEN YOUR ENTRY AND YOUR PROTECTIVE STOP. YOU CAN ACCOMPLISH THIS WHEN ENTERING AT OR NEAR THE CONTROL PRICE OR THE VALUE LIMITS. YOU WILL HAVE AS BARRIER FOR YOUR PROTECTIVE STOP, THE TAIL OF THE REJECTION AND THE CONTROL PRICE, VALUE HIGH OR VALUE LOW

10. IN A HORIZONTAL VALUE AREA, TAILS, TRADING ACTIVITY AND INITIATIVE MOVEMENTS CAN BE ON BOTH SIDES OF VALUE. THIS IS NOT NECESSARILY A REQUIREMENT, BUT, WHEN YOU DO SEE TAILS BELOW THE HORIZONTAL VALUE, MORE TRADING ACTIVITY ON THE TOP HALF OF THE VALUE AREA AND MORE BUYING INITIATIVE MOVEMENTS THAN SELLING ONES, IT WOULD BE PREFERABLE TO LOOK FOR A BUYING OPPORTUNITY ONLY IN ORDER TO HAVE THE ODDS IN YOUR FAVOR. IF THE SITUATION CHANGES AND YOU SEE THE SELLERS PICK UP THE PACE, THEN YOU CAN LOOK FOR SELLING OPPORTUNITIES TOO

11. IN UPTREND, HAVE THE SELLERS MADE A RECENT TAIL ABOVE VALUE AND CURRENTLY PRICE IS MAKING NARROW ROTATIONS BETWEEN THE CONTROL AND THE VALUE LOW? DO NOT BUY. THE UPTREND LOOKS LIKE IT IS ABOUT TO END. IF IT DOES END, WAIT FOR PRICE TO DEVELOP A LOWER VALUE AND START LOOKING FOR THE NEW CONTROL. IF IT DOES NOT BREAK THE VALUE BUT RESUMES PRICE ROTATIONS BETWEEN UPPER AND LOWER LIMITS OF THE BIG UPTREND VALUE, RESUME BUYING FROM EXCESS BELOW VALUE TO JUST ABOVE THE CONTROL AND SELLING ABOVE VALUE IN EXCESS TERRITORY

12. IN DOWNTREND, IF BUYERS HAVE MADE A STRONG RECENT TAIL BELOW VALUE AND CURRENT PRICE ROTATIONS ARE

NOW CONFINED BETWEEN THE CONTROL AND VALUE HIGH, DO NOT SELL. THE DOWNTREND IS ENDING. IF IT DOES END, BREAKING VALUE AREA HIGH AND DEVELOPING A HIGHER VALUE PRECEDED BY A BUYING INITIATIVE MOVE, START LOOKING FOR THE NEW CONTROL. IF SOMEHOW, THE DOWNTREND DOES NOT END BUT RESUMES COMPLETE ROTATIONS FROM THE VALUE HIGH TO THE VALUE LOW AND BACK, RETURN TO NORMAL TRADING BEHAVIOR IN A DOWNTREND. SELL FROM EXCESS ABOVE VALUE TO JUST BELOW THE CONTROL AND BUY IN EXCESS BELOW VALUE

13. IN HORIZONTAL VALUE AREA, IF SELLERS HAVE MADE A RECENT TAIL ABOVE VALUE AND CURRENT PRICE ROTATIONS ARE SITUATED IN THE LOWER HALF OF THE VALUE AREA, DO NOT BUY. THE SELLERS HAVE WON THE WAR AND THE VALUE IS GOING TO BRAKE TO THE DOWNSIDE

14. IN THE SAME HORIZONTAL VALUE AREA, IF BUYERS MADE A RECENT TAIL BELOW VALUE AND PRICE ROTATIONS ARE CURRENTLY DEVELOPING BETWEEN THE CONTROL AND VALUE HIGH, DO NOT SELL. THE VALUE IS ABOUT TO BRAKE TO THE UPSIDE

15. WHEN IN UPTREND OR DOWNTREND, IF PRICE DEVELOPS ONE OF THE THREE VALUE TYPES THAT WILL USUALLY

SIGNAL THE END OF A TREND, AS DISCUSSED IN THE "TREND CHANGE" SECTION, STOP TRADING ACTIVITY UNTIL YOU HAVE CONFIRMATION THAT EITHER THE TREND HAS BEEN BROKEN OR, IT WILL CONTINUE. FIND SOMETHING ELSE TO TRADE IN THIS PERIOD. THERE WILL BE PLENTY FOR YOU TO CHOOSE FROM.

Carefully read these guidelines. Write them on a piece of paper if you want until you get used to them and refer to them before taking any trading decision.

SUPPLY AND DEMAND KEY LEVELS

I have discussed a lot about supply and demand throughout this book and how we can see the footprint of the long term buyer and seller entering the market. It is now time to take advantage of this knowledge and identify very strong supply and demand price levels in the market that we are actually going to trade.

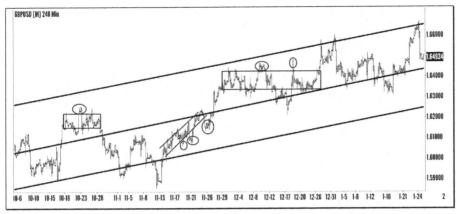

FIGURE 44: SUPPLY AND DEMAND LEVELS INSIDE THE VALUE AREA

Notice above that there are three diagonal lines that cross the entire chart from left to right. Those are the markings of the value area on the higher timeframe with the one in the middle being the control price, of course.

See the rectangles inside the value area. Those are small value areas. 2 above control and one below. There are more value areas there as you can see. I just drew the ones we are more interested in with respect to finding supply and demand zones.

Observe the tails and excess of each of these three value areas. Those are all marked with circles. You do not need to draw the rectangles on your charts at this point to engulf the small value areas inside the big value.

I drew them in order to make the excess and tails more visible.

But you will see them without the need of rectangles. When you see a price spike that protrudes outside from the surrounding slow moving price, you will easily recognize it as a tail.

The surrounding slow moving, or sideways moving price would be the small value. The tail is the footprint of buyers or sellers entering the market. Let's see the same chart again but with more emphasis on the tails this time.

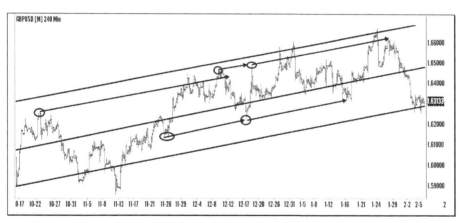

FIGURE 45: SUPPLY AND DEMAND MOVING AT THE SAME PACE WITH CONTROL

See how easy it becomes to find out where future price will be stopping and turning. The supply and demand areas, move in line with the control price. Drawing a line from the tail onwards, parallel with the control price will reveal future supply and demand levels that we can trade. Observe how price finds strong support or resistance at these levels in the market, that we have discovered a long before the price has actually arrived there.

See how price touched these levels and then changed direction. All you need to do now is get used to them on your charts. Draw the control price on a timeframe, then go to a lower timeframe of the same chart and find the tails above and below the control. The bigger the tail, the stronger the demand or supply at that level. Draw, starting from this tail, a perfectly parallel line with control price, extending it further to the right of the chart. Watch what happens when future price action makes its way to this extended line. Also, notice that on the first tail from the left, in the bottom half of the value area, there are another two tails close below it.

This is a very strong demand zone with buying orders all over the place. Naturally, we go to a lower timeframe and we wait for price to show rejection of one of those levels. In this situation, price rejects the first tail that comes into its path.

PRICE ACTION BREAKDOWN

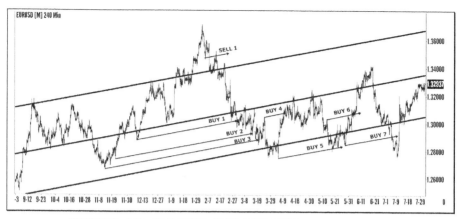

FIGURE 46: BUYING AND SELLING IN UPTREND

See how every time price reacts on each extension in line with the control of the demand areas, in the bottom half of the value. As price comes down towards the value low, many buying opportunities arise. One by one, as price reaches them, you go to a lower timeframe to enter the trade if price will show rejection of the demand zone. Remember that rejection is a value area with one or more tails piercing the demand level. Refer to the "rejection" section of the book and to "Figure 39". This is an uptrend so, after we have done the value area analysis on the higher timeframe, as long as the trend is healthy and is respecting the "guidelines" mentioned earlier, we seek to buy in the area from excess price below value to just above the control price. We seek to sell in the excess area above value. Notice on "buy 4" and "buy 6" how price comes from below. These tails act as a resistance for price at first.

We are not interested in selling the rejection of resistance because there is an uptrend in place. We only sell above value in excess territory. In the bottom half of the value of the uptrend we need to buy. So we wait to see what happens with price around these levels. If they get passed to the upside, they will now be acting as support for price. We go to the lower timeframe to see the rejection of what is now a support level. We proceed to enter a buy order as described in the section about rejection and on "Figure 39". The take profit level for the buy orders and the sell order will naturally be the control price.

At the "buy 3" order, you can see that price did not manage to go all the way to the control price to hit our profit level. You will, of course, manage every trade from beginning to the end, do not leave the protective stop at its initial place. When the trade moves into profit, move your protective stop into profit as well, but under logical levels where the price will have very much trouble getting at. Those levels would be the small tails that price will make on the lower timeframe where you entered the trade, on its way up to the trade exit level.

In an uptrend, when you buy in excess below value or somewhere in the bottom half of the value area, the take profit level is always at the control price. When an opportunity arises to buy just above the control, the take profit will be at the value high. The protective stop will always be below the tail of the smaller rejection value area on the lower timeframe that is used to enter the trade. The risk will always be smaller than the reward unless you are buying extremely close below the control price. If you find yourself in such a situation where the risk would be greater than the potential reward, do not take the trade. As you will see, these type of trades will often times have a potential reward at least twice the size of the risk you will be taking.

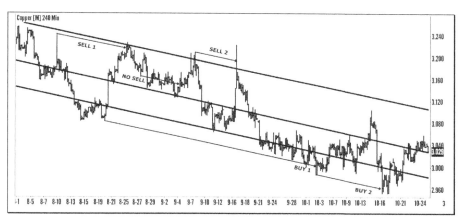

FIGURE 47: BUYING AND SELLING IN DOWNTREND

In the chart above there is a selling opportunity there between "sell 1" and "sell 2" that you should not take, even if it meets all the criteria and you see a rejection on the lower timeframe. You would have to set your protective stop above the tail of the rejection. You can clearly see from this chart, without looking at the lower timeframe that the risk would be roughly the same size as the reward. Do not sell. At "sell 2" you can see a selling opportunity in excess above value. The same as with all trades, go to a lower timeframe, wait for the rejection, enter the trade at the retest of value low of the small rejection, and set protective stop just above the big tail seen on this chart. Take profit at the control price. Selling above value gives you the greatest risk-reward ratio as you can see. At "buy 1" and "buy 2" we are in excess price below value in a downtrend.

These are also great trades that offer very low risk and high reward. Price, almost, can't go any lower as we are already in a downtrend and it has gone below value. It will have to start trading vertically down to go lower than that which is highly unlikely in a healthy trend. The take profit is at the control price and the protective stop will be trailed in profit under tails of the small timeframe that showed rejection.

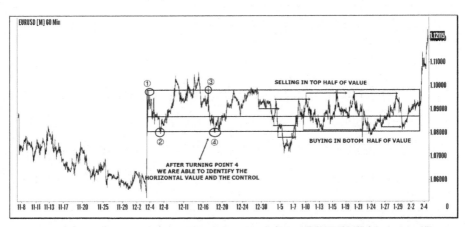

FIGURE 48: BUYING AND SELLING IN HORIZONTAL VALUE

As you can see, after price prints the "4" swing we can already identify the horizontal value. We see its excess between points "1" and "2" and we see its control roughly in the middle of it. We then move on to find trading setups. We sell in the top value area or above value and we buy in the bottom value area or below value. We enter each trade after rejection on a lower timeframe and as long as the risk is smaller than the reward.

This is very recent price action on the EURUSD currency pair. Most of these trades I took myself. Before each trade, I am going to stress once again that you need to have the guidelines in front of you, at least until you get used to this type of trading.

CLOSING WORDS

Please take the time to read the material as many times as you have to. Do not rush into trading without a clear understanding of the contents. Read each chapter, practice, read, practice. If you are new to trading and it sounds confusing at first, do not give up. Take some time off, come back and read it again. Do all the practice and more. Make thorough analysis of every concept and idea described in this book. Do not just take my word for it. Maybe you can manage to draw even more efficient conclusions than I did after extensive chart studying.

Depending on what timeframe you are going to use for trading, you will see many of these setups on your charts, regardless of what market you are trading. Keep in mind that, as with any trading method, the higher the timeframe you are trading on, the better your overall results will be.

The higher the timeframe, the less noise it has and the least susceptible you are to erratic moves as a result of fundamental news. I have been trading like described above in the last two years, more or less, and the outcome has been very good for me. I do lose a trade from time to time, but most of the times that is as a result of news generated volatility that makes price create spikes in the market.

Often times, these spikes touch your protective stop only to reverse and go straight to what would have been your take profit level. This is upsetting. To avoid this as much as possible, try to set your protective stop a little bit lower or higher than you would have set it logically, just below or above the tail. Do this especially if you intend to trade on low timeframes. Take the time to learn the contents of this book, you will be congratulating yourself later that you did. Reading the price action is by far the most effective way to trade and make profits month after month.

In the end, I would like to state once again that English is not my native language.

Therefore, if you happen to come across some confusing passages when reading this book, please do not hesitate to contact me at laurentiudamir@gmail.com. Do this if you have any questions regarding the contents of the book in general, not just about my English language skills. I will reply as soon as I get the time. Unfortunately, I do not have any complementary products to sell you into at the end of this book. ☺. This was irony of course. I am a trader, I do not have any websites to sell some magical formulas or indicators about trading. To be honest, I do not have any desire in doing that anytime soon.

If you would be so kind to take five minutes of your time and write a review of the book, sharing your thoughts with other people, that would be very much appreciated. Thank you for taking the time to read the book. I trust it will add value to your trading.

Made in the USA
Monee, IL
21 April 2020